WHO ARE THE BAPTISTS?

Even before the thunder of the Reformation rumbled across the world, brave Christians were looking for the liberty to worship God as they freely chose.

These were the spiritual forefathers of the Baptists, the champions of freedom who have helped shape not only Protestantism but the very fabric of Western thought and government.

In the tradition of Roger Williams, William Carey, and Adoniram Judson, the author of this book highlights what all Baptists hold in common:
- freedom of conscience
- the primacy of the Scriptures
- the need for personal commitment to Christ
- the call to evangelism

This is a book not only about great men and women of the past but about a living, thriving body of believers—North and South, black and white, young and old, rural and urban—who seek to be Christ's people in the 20th century.

The Baptist Heritage

Edward B. Cole

David C. Cook Publishing Co.
ELGIN, ILLINOIS—WESTON, ONTARIO
LA HABRA, CALIFORNIA

THE BAPTIST HERITAGE
Copyright © 1976 David C. Cook Publishing Co.

All rights reserved. Except for brief excerpts for review purposes, no part of this book may be reproduced or used in any form or by any means—electronic or mechanical, including photocopying, recording, or information storage and retrieval systems—without written permission from the publisher.

David C. Cook Publishing Co., Elgin, IL 60120

Printed in the United States of America
Library of Congress Catalog Number: 76-11915

ISBN: 0-89191-055-7

Special acknowledgment is made to the Christian Literature Crusade for permission to use the poem "Gold Cord" by Amy Carmichael.

CONTENTS

Foreword — 7
Preface — 9

PART I: History
1. *The Early History* — 13
2. *The Fire Kindles* — 20
3. *Spreading to the American Colonies* — 30
4. *Expanding the Borders* — 39
5. *Into All the World* — 52

PART II: Beliefs
6. *The People of a Book* — 69
7. *A Gospel That Changes Persons* — 78
8. *Members of a Body* — 98
9. *Popes, Pastors, and Presbyters* — 111
10. *A Freedom-Loving People* — 131

PART III: Ministry
11. *Evangelistic Involvement* — 145
12. *Missionary Outreach* — 160
13. *Christian Education* — 176
14. *Social Ministry* — 186
Appendix — 201

Foreword

DR. EDWARD COLE HAS WRITTEN a helpful study of the Baptist movement. I know it will be an inspiration to many people, whether they are Baptists or not.

This book is not simply a cold, impersonal chronicle of dates and names. It is instead an intensely inspiring history of the people and ideas which have shaped the Baptist tradition and made it the largest single segment of Protestantism today.

Baptists have made many significant contributions to the American nation. Their emphasis on individualism, as Dr. Cole shows, has had a positive influence on American democracy. Baptists have also given guidance and inspiration to other Christian denominations by their zeal and pioneering spirit. As this book points out, Baptists have often been in the forefront of missions. It was a Baptist,

William Carey, who became the father of the modern missionary movement. Adding their hands were other famous missionary Baptists like Adoniram Judson, Luther Rice, and John Mason Peck.

Of particular interest to me is the importance Baptists have always given to evangelism and conversion. Who knows what the outreach of churches throughout the world would be if all Christian believers adopted the Baptist thesis that "everything we do ought to be evangelistic"?

The Baptist Heritage is a saga of obedience to the Word of God that will challenge and benefit many Christians. It can help us all to pause, to be inspired by the commitment of the past, to gain new strength from the Gospel, and to redouble our efforts for an aggressive world-wide witness for Christ.

BILLY GRAHAM

Preface

IT HAS GIVEN ME JOY TO WRITE these chapters about the Baptists. There have been moments of apprehension, however, lest anyone misunderstand the intent of such a book. In writing about the Baptists I have sought to enunciate some of those characteristics and qualities that God has used to bless many people down through the centuries. By no means are these qualities exclusively the property of the Baptists. Our sister denominations have also had their significant characteristics and qualities. Yet, there is a distinctiveness to the Baptist contribution which needs to be periodically stated with humility and candor.

Unfortunately, Baptists are as capable of being small-minded and bigoted as anyone. To deny this is to encourage an unhealthy self-conceit that God's Spirit could not bless. My thoughts join with the renowned Walter Rauschenbusch (1861-1918), Baptist preacher and professor of many years, when he says:

> I do not want to make Baptists shut themselves up in their little clamshells and be indifferent to the ocean outside of them. I am a Baptist, but I am more than a Baptist. All things are mine; whether Francis of Assisi, or Luther or Knox, or Wesley; all are mine because I am Christ's. The old Adam is a strict denominationalist; the new Adam is just a Christian.

It is in this spirit that I have sought to present the Baptist picture in three parts. *Part I* is devoted to a historical presentation of those persons, places and things that have made Baptist history. *Part II* is a limited delineation of Baptist doctrine and its impact upon the Baptist movement. *Part III* is an attempt to encapsulate this history and doctrine into a statement of life-style that might be generally accepted by the rank-and-file Baptist constituency. We have sought to show the glories and foibles of this amazing people called "the Baptists" as they have attempted to follow what they saw as the teachings of their Lord through bad times and good.

EDWARD B. COLE

PART I: History

1

The Early History

BAPTISTS! WHO ARE THEY? Where did they come from? How did they acquire their name? They certainly did not select it, nor did their forebears. It was hurled at them in scorn and derision; but, as with other epithets given in similar circumstances, it has won respect and honor over the years.

The people who have borne that name have left a fascinating trail of character and movement that has led to the development of what we now know as "Baptist" churches. While their roots can be traced back to pre-Reformation days, the actual use of the name "Baptist" is not found in English literature until the year 1644 when the Particular Baptists used it in their first confession of faith.

There have been some Baptists who have asserted a kind of apostolic succession, or, if you will, a direct line from the present back to the days of John the Baptist. Their theory has been smilingly referred to as the "John-Jordan-Jerusalem Theory." But it is historically unwarranted and undocumented.

More credibly, others find the Baptist origins in the Anabaptist and Mennonite movements of Europe. However, the weight of scholarship favors English Congregationalism in the 17th century as the true starting point. In any event, the better part of wisdom would suggest that both influences made significant contributions to the development of the Baptists.

The early history of this people manifests daring, romance, vision, and courage. It is a saga of seeking freedom of soul and conscience with the right to worship God as the individual conscience and understanding dictated. This soul-freedom has become a key to the history of the Baptists.

It was their conviction that every man and woman has both the ability and the need to enter directly into a saving relationship with God through Jesus Christ. No outside mediation is necessary. Baptists determinedly resisted anything that repressed such freedom. Their long, hard struggle included costly sacrifices, even death, for their beliefs. By thus being willing to pay the ultimate price, they, consciously and unconsciously, affirmed their spiritual kinship with those early heroes of the faith whose stories are recorded on the pages of the New Testament.

In Acts 2:41-47, the earliest Christians are described as a people who had known Jesus Christ and

The Early History

believed in Him soon after His crucifixion and resurrection. They were meeting in homes and small groups, but were united in one common bond of faith in Jesus. There was no fixed organization with priests, bishops, ritual, or church buildings, as we know them. Rather, the early believers looked to the authoritative leadership of first the Apostles, and then an emerging, simple administrative structure to further the objectives of faith delivered by Christ to His Apostles.

As, through the following centuries, an established church developed, there existed alongside it and, periodically, within it a nonconformist minority who rejected the accumulating tradition. They preached openly from the Bible and declared that the Scriptures ought to be given the place of primacy and authority over all men, councils, or popes. They spoke out against the sacramental system as unbiblical and inept as a means of salvation. They taught that Biblical baptism followed a vital, personal acceptance of Christ by faith, thus precluding infant baptism. In short, they sought to return to the purity and simplicity of the church as it was portrayed in the Book of Acts.

This nonconformist attitude grew and, in the 12th century, began to assume significant proportions. Even within the established church, cries for reform were heard. Many of the leaders of the popular movements were imprisoned, banished, tortured, or burned at the stake for their uncompromising stand.

THE BAPTIST HERITAGE

Yet even in their death new followers emerged, and new leaders took up the cry for change. The stage was being set for the Protestant Reformation of the 16th century.

Some of the voices crying out prior to the Reformation were men like Peter of Bruys. We know little about him except for what we find in the writings of his enemies who spoke of his repudiation of infant baptism, the veneration of the cross, and other practices of the established church. He was burned at the stake in 1140 A.D.

Arnold of Brescia was another voice who helped set the stage for the Baptist movement as he decried the political maneuverings, the pomposity, and the carnality of the church. He was hanged, his body burned, and his ashes thrown into the Tiber River in 1155 A.D.

Peter Waldo, whose followers took the name "Waldensians," was surely another forerunner. He opposed any authority for the church other than that of the sacred Scriptures, and taught that no man had the right to be mediator between man and God. He held that God must be obeyed over the edicts of popes, priests, bishops or councils.

Martin Luther nailed his famous Ninety-five Theses to the door of the Castle Church in Wittenburg on October 31, 1517, opening the period of the Reformation. With Luther in Germany, Zwingli in Switzerland, and John Calvin in France, the Reformation found its most articulate advocates and teachers.

The Early History

Their writings, their great sermons, their burning hearts bequeathed new hope to the souls of men.

Others followed in their train, such as Balthasar Hubmaier who held it to be blasphemy "to teach that any kind of images can draw our souls to piety." He spoke against infant baptism, and taught that the Mass was unscriptural because the Lord's Supper was a memorial for believers, and not a sacrifice to be offered by priests. His teachings and leadership gave direction and definition to the Anabaptist movement in Europe. He was so hated that the Catholic church burned him at the stake in Vienna in 1528.

The list of the Baptists' spiritual kindred could be a very long one indeed. The Anabaptists, so-called because of their insistence upon re-baptizing new believers even though they had undergone infant baptism, must also be numbered in the list of forerunners of the Baptists.

In 1524, delegates from various Anabaptist groups gathered in the Austrian village of Waldshut to compare their interpretations of Scripture and to draw up a plan of separation from the Catholic church. This was a historic hour. They formulated their stance and drew up articles about baptism stating that it must be preceded by faith, and then issued a "Directory for Christian Living." The Waldshut conference helped to lay further foundations for the Baptist movement.

The Anabaptists were soon to be severely dealt

with by civil authorities, as well as the Catholic church. Even other Protestant bodies who feared their stance on infant baptism and democratic principles treated them very harshly. Hubmaier was tortured by Zwingli, for example, and Servetus burned in Geneva. But the persecution merely spread their ranks throughout Europe. Some of the Anabaptists migrated to Holland where they were to become known as Mennonites. From Holland the concepts of the Anabaptists would find their way to England, and be influential in the course of the Reformation there.

The term "Protestant" was not used during the Reformation, nor for years afterward. But it is essentially an accurate description. Its primary meaning is not negative, but rather has positive overtones. The term comes from the Latin *protestari: pro* meaning "forth" and *testari* meaning "to call to witness." The Reformers were not merely protesting; they were speaking loudly and clearly for what they saw as a viable, Biblical, personal faith in Jesus Christ.

Certainly the Reformation was not originally a plan to break away from the church, but a movement to reform it from within. However, there were forces—national, political, spiritual, and intellectual—that had been building like dark thunderclouds on the European horizon. The winds of Reformation swept the storm across Europe, gathering the forces and focusing them in the person of an Augustinian monk, Martin Luther. When the storm

The Early History

cleared, the shape of Christendom had been changed forever.

Questions for Thought and Discussion

1. "Soul-freedom" is defined by the author as "the ability and the need to enter directly into a saving relationship with God through Jesus Christ." Why is this a key to Baptist history?
2. Why did the nonconformist minority reject the "accumulating tradition" and the "sacramental system" during the first 12 centuries of church growth? Were they always right in doing so?
3. Why is it that individuals who set out to reform the church are so often persecuted, abused, and even killed by its officials?
4. For the average church-goer, the Bible is received and understood through the interpretation of a pastor or teacher. How does this affect the principle of "sola Scriptura"? How does the Protestant position differ from the Catholic?
5. What do we mean when we say that Martin Luther changed the shape of Christendom?

Suggestions for Further Study

Robert G. Torbet, *A History of the Baptists,* 3rd ed. (Valley Forge: Judson Press, 1975), pp. 17-32.

2

The Fire Kindles

THE REFORMATION CAME TO ENGLAND through a complex mixture of political maneuvering and religious insight. The line between the two was not always clearly drawn.

The occasion for the break with Rome came when Pope Clement VII refused to recognize Henry VIII's divorce from his wife, Catherine, and his marriage to Anne Boleyn.

Catherine had only one child who lived, a daughter, Mary. From Henry's point of view, the divorce and remarriage were necessary in order to provide a male heir to the throne and thus insure the stability of government. (The only other occasion in English history when a woman had tried to rule had provoked the disastrous Wars of Succession.)

The pope's refusal to recognize Henry's marriage

The Fire Kindles

was not based on morality or Scripture. He was dominated politically by the Spanish emperor, Charles V, who was Catherine's nephew. The pope could only recognize the divorce with Charles' approval; yet if Charles approved he would damage his aunt's reputation—which he would not do. At its simplest, England's affairs of state were being dictated by the Spanish government.

This was intolerable to Henry, and the rising tide of nationalism supported him. So the relationship with Rome was severed in 1534. While the church remained Catholic, Henry replaced the pope as its head.

Behind this political confrontation with Rome were other factors paving the way for the creation of the Church of England. Not the least of these was the preaching and example of Wycliffe, a full century and a half before Henry maneuvered Parliament into declaring him the head of his national church. The principle of "sola Scriptura" (the Scriptures only), which became the rallying cry of the Reformation, was clearly taught by Wycliffe. In open defiance of Rome, he translated the major portion of the Bible into English, and advocated a return to Biblical simplicity. Though he was eventually forbidden to preach, and his followers were persecuted, nevertheless, the seed had been sown.

Another factor was the impact of the learning of the Renaissance on the concept of papal authority. Many of the documents upon which the pope's authority had been based were proven beyond a shadow of a doubt to be forgeries, some from as late as the ninth century. With the basis for the papal claim to authority so severely undermined, what need had England then to bow to Rome?

A further factor was the boost in communication that came with the invention of the printing press. Knowledge and information were reaching more people and faster than ever before. Erasmus' sly parodies of the foibles of church and priesthood were pointing out the need for change. Luther's writings were widely disseminated and were very influential in England; by the time of Henry's break with Rome perhaps 50 percent of the English bishops leaned toward "Lutheranism."

The break with Rome, however, did little to ease the position of the nonconformists. Throughout the remainder of the sixteenth century, including the reigns of the first Queen Elizabeth and James I, the form of worship and faith was predetermined for the people of England.

However, the fires were kindling! A smoldering resentment was venting itself. People were questioning the authority of the Anglican Church, as well as their monarch, in matters of conscience. Inevitably, conflicts arose and resulted in political and economic sanctions, and even death for the nonconformists. These were years of grave personal danger for those intrepid souls who dared question authority, national morality, or the tendentious theology prescribed by

The Fire Kindles

the monarchs of England and their loyal prelates.

The attempts for reform within Anglicanism were judged insufficient by those who were becoming known as Puritans. For the most part, Puritans wished to remain within the Church of England and purify it. Yet there were some who were impatient at the conservative attitude of the church leaders and they withdrew into independent organizations. These became known as the Separatists.

The Separatists did not believe that the Anglican Church was holding to Scriptural practices, and they rejected its authority over the local congregation. The only authority they would recognize was the Scripture itself.

In 1606 a young man in poor health came to the home of Separatists Thomas and Jane Helwys. He was made welcome and considered part of their family. The young man was John Smyth, an intellectually curious Cambridge graduate with a deep commitment to the authority of the Bible.

In 1600 he had been appointed pastor of the Lincoln Church, but because of his nonconformist views and life-style he had been removed from his position by the authorities. He had agonized for months in prayer and study prior to his decision to leave Anglicanism. Upon making his decision, broken in body and spirit, he had sought fellowship with Thomas and Jane Helwys who were meeting with other families for Bible study and prayer in Gainsborough.

THE BAPTIST HERITAGE

A few miles down the road, in the manor of Scrooby, there was yet another group of Separatists who felt close affinity to their friends in Gainsborough. Within the Scrooby congregation were William Bradford, William Brewster and John Robinson.

At this time King James I was zealously carrying out his threat: "I will make them conform, or I will harry them out of the land." The growing violence, persecution, and harassment caused the Separatists to despair for their existence. They were indeed "harried" from the land.

Helwys and Smyth, harassed and wearied, emigrated to Holland in 1609 with their small congregation of 37 souls. Once in Amsterdam, John Smyth poured[1] water over himself and others in baptism. In that act of commitment the first English-speaking Baptist church was formed. It is in this tiny congregation, gathered in Amsterdam, Holland, that most Baptists find the roots of their denomination.

It was not long after the Gainsborough congregation under Helwys and Smyth had emigrated to Amsterdam that the Scrooby congregation under John Robinson also emigrated to Holland, traveling through Amsterdam and on to Leyden. This, with certain additions, was to become the congregation

[1] Pouring was a common form in his day. However, shortly thereafter the Baptists of England in their study of Scripture discovered that the Greek word *baptizo* meant "immerse, to dip, to put under." Immersion then became the normative mode of baptism.

The Fire Kindles

which would ultimately board the *Mayflower* as the Pilgrims who came to the shores of America in 1620.

Among the beliefs held dear by the congregation associated with Helwys and Smyth was that of the church being a gathered group of believers who had been baptized in the name of the Father and the Son and the Holy Spirit. They further asserted their individual right to worship God according to their own conscience without dictates from the king or state. They emphasized the dignity of persons and the absolute liberty, in the realm of the Spirit, of each soul to choose his own mode of worship. Such a clarion call to religious freedom echoes down the corridors of history and is expressed in our own Constitution and the documents of all democratic bodies.

As the small band of believers progressed in their studies of Scripture in Holland they sensed differences of opinion developing among themselves regarding the relation of church authority and baptism. The differences, while discussed in love, were nonetheless real. Helwys and Smyth sadly took leave of one another, a portion of the congregation going with each man. Smyth moved closer to the position of the Mennonites with whom he seemed to be more comfortable, and Helwys and some eight or ten men and women returned to Spitalfield (just outside of London), England, where he established what history confirms as the first Baptist church on English soil.

Worshiping in secret began to grate on Helwys. After one year of clandestine worship Helwys decided to stir the spiritual embers into a flame, openly, whatever the cost, and declare his faith to all men including his king.

In 1612, Thomas Helwys published a small book entitled *A Short Description of the Mistery of Iniquity*. In it he challenged the monarch's right to determine the form or content of how individuals would worship God. He knew he risked imprisonment or death for his views, but a fire burned in his soul that had to be expressed. He set out to have an audience with King James, carrying a copy of his book with an inscription in the front that read:

> Heare O King, and dispise not ye counsell of ye poor, and let their complaints come before thee. The King is mortall man and not God, therefore hath no power over ye immortall souls of his subjects, to make laws and ordinances for them.

The response of the king was predictable. He ordered Helwys summarily sent to prison. From that day nothing was ever again heard of Thomas Helwys.

Many great personalities were to emerge from this conflagration in England. Truths were being vindicated and the superficialities of a banal formalism were effectively being challenged by men such as John Bunyan (1628-1688), the Baptist preacher of Bedford. His timeless allegory, *The Pilgrim's Prog-*

The Fire Kindles

ress, was written during his 12-year stay in a Bedford prison. Bunyan was imprisoned with the provision that he might have his freedom at any time if he would agree to "cease preaching." He tenaciously refused to make such a promise saying, "I can suffer for my Lord, but I cannot deny Him." Fortunately, the Act of Toleration in 1689 relieved the Baptists from the fear of punishment for following their Christian convictions. While this Act did not remove all problems that would attend building a free church within England, it did essentially give these early Baptists the encouragement to seek their own destiny under God.

In the same year (1689) an assembly of Baptists was called in London. They adopted most of the Westminster Confession, formulated some 46 years earlier by other Christians. Only a few deletions or alterations were made in those chapters that had to do with church polity, ordinances, and civil magistrates. This significant move on the part of English Baptists revealed that, as far as possible, they wanted to be in harmony with other Christians.

These early Baptists were a plain, middle-class folk, although many of their ministers were educated men. They used plain language; called their churches "meeting houses"; gave their women equal privileges with men; refused to give stated salaries to their ministers, but gave voluntarily to them; fasted; washed each other's feet; anointed the sick with oil; excommunicated their members if they

THE BAPTIST HERITAGE

married "out of the Meeting"; kept a strict discipline over their members and looked upon all amusements with disfavor. Gradually, however, they moved away from some of their more peculiar practices and a steadier growth resulted.

A prominent Baptist preacher who built upon the work of these courageous forebears was William Carey (1761-1834). Carey lived the Great Commission of Matthew 28: 19, 20. He committed himself to the spreading of the Gospel to other lands. Much of the widespread missionary activity among Baptists stems from his ministry and vision which culminated in 1792 in the English Baptist Missionary Society. He became its first missionary to India and started the modern missionary movement as we know it today among English-speaking peoples.

The well-loved Robert Hall (1764-1831) pastored in Cambridge and Bristol. His oratory and compassionate spirit were lauded throughout England.

Charles Haddon Spurgeon (1834-1892), who served many years as pastor of the Metropolitan Tabernacle in London, became a great spokesman for Baptists both in England and America.

These are but a few of the great names that arose from the early English Baptists, whose fires of conviction were so thoroughly kindled that they quite literally leaped across the ocean to the new continent of America.

Questions for Thought and Discussion

1. What, in your estimation, was the most important cause of England's break with Rome? Why?
2. Remembering the often grim government repressions in Church history, what would you consider to be the ideal relationship between Church and State? How much control, if any, should the state have over church affairs?
3. When the English rejected the authority of the pope, what took its place? Why didn't this ease the pressure on the nonconformists?
4. How does the idea of the church as a "gathered group of believers" differ from the Anglican or Roman Catholic position?
5. Is the Scripture clear on the ideal form of church government? Justify your answer.
6. What did Thomas Helwys accomplish by taking his book to the King? What would you have done in his place?
7. Describe the similarities between the persecution of the Separatists by King James I and the persecution of the early Christians in Acts 8—9? What differences are there?

Suggestions for Further Study

Winthrop S. Hudson, "By Way of Perspective," *Baptist Concepts of the Church*, ed. W. S. Hudson (Philadelphia: Judson Press, 1959), pp. 11-17.

2. Torbet, *A History of the Baptists*, pp. 33-43.

3

Spreading To The American Colonies

WITH THE LANDING OF THE PILGRIMS at Plymouth in 1620, the beginnings of a new colony were under way. The settlement was soon augmented by another group of people, the well-known Puritans, who desired to reform the Anglican Church from all connections with Rome in terms of liturgical rites, prayer books, beads, and state control. Ironically, these two groups merged at last to form a Congregational Church that became, in some ways, a replica of the Anglican Church, including enforced taxation and government by a state-church combination of authority. The enigma lay in the fact that these men and women who had risked life and limb to find freedom of worship, having once gained their freedom in the colonies, promptly refused to accept it for themselves and abrasively denied it to others who migrated later. So it was that the Massachusetts Bay

Spreading to the American Colonies

Colony developed. To this colony came the man who was destined to be known for years to come as the "father of religious liberty in America," Roger Williams.

Williams had taken his studies at Cambridge, England, like some of the other colonists. He had been a brilliant student showing great promise as a preacher-teacher of the Gospel. During his student days he had heard of the barbarities perpetrated in the name of justice on a Scottish doctor and minister, Alexander Leighton, who had been indicted and tried for nonconformity. The sentence meted out was a 10,000-pound fine and facial disfigurement: ears severed, nose slit and face branded. Roger Williams could not forget that kind of justice. Archbishop William Laud, a pawn of King Charles I, publicly expressed thanks to God for the hideous sentence handed down to Leighton. (Later Laud also became a victim of disfavor with the king and was beheaded.) It was this Archbishop who created the situation forcing Williams, after speaking against oppression and religious conformity, to leave England at age 28.

February 5, 1631, found the good ship *Lyon* dropping anchor in Boston's harbor after an exhausting two-month voyage from England. There were 20 passengers aboard including Roger and his wife, Mary Barnard Williams. Putting into port, they could see that Boston was a tiny settlement of cabins situated on a few hills. The town's center was a cow pasture and the streets were muddy paths created by

THE BAPTIST HERITAGE

men and their animals. While the town looked dismal to them, the fires of hope and freedom burned in their hearts.

At the time of Roger Williams' arrival in America there were only two significant colonies there, one at Jamestown, Virginia, and another in Salem, Massachusetts. Jamestown had been founded in 1607 by the Cavaliers or Royalists of England who had brought their Anglican forms of worship to the new world. The colony in Massachusetts was composed of Puritans and Separatists who had united to form the Congregational Church.

Early in April the people of Salem sought Williams' services as their pastor. They had glowing reports of his abilities and needed a preacher since their own had died. Williams felt this was God's will for him and he accepted the call. Immediately, trouble beset him. He began to speak boldly against the practices of punishing negligent attenders at Sunday worship. The Civil Magistrates, in his view, were the last ones to be given the authority to enforce church discipline and punish religious offenders. So he sarcastically attacked the system and was immediately in open conflict with the civic and religious leaders. Such pressure built up in the community that Williams stole away to Plymouth where he hoped to find greater freedom and a more receptive audience. Here, for two years, he lived and taught, winning many to his views. He began a mission to the Indian tribes, developed an Indian

Spreading to the American Colonies

dictionary, and made lasting friendships.

However, when he received an invitation to return to Salem, in spite of the obvious risks he went back and again began challenging the authority of church-state control. He openly advocated complete separation of the two. Earlier in Plymouth he had written a searing paper against the king's declaration that he had the right to give away land belonging originally to the Indians without purchasing it from them. To his enemies, his paper smacked not only of heresy but of treason. The authorities demanded he recant, but he refused.

In October of 1635 he was summoned before a court consisting of the governor, the deputy governor, eight assistants and 25 deputies. Four charges were leveled at Williams. They focused on his contentions that: the civil power had no rights over a man's conscience; the settlers themselves had no right to deal unfairly with the Indians in taking over their land; the people were to blame for not separating from the Anglican Church. Roger Williams stood that day and said, "I am ready to be bound and banished and even to die in New England rather than renounce my opinions." For this, the court sentenced him to banishment, but due to his wife's advanced pregnancy and his own poor health they allowed him to return to his home in Salem. He was welcomed home by his friends and, with all the notoriety he had gained, larger crowds than ever before attended his preaching. The authorities were

THE BAPTIST HERITAGE

frightened and plotted to seize him and deport him to England. A band of armed men actually sailed from Boston to Salem by boat to capture Williams, but when they arrived Williams was gone. He had escaped to his Indian friends while his wife Mary was tended by neighbors who had secretly taken her into their home.

We must keep in mind that Salem was the Colony to which settlers had come for religious freedom. They had been harassed and persecuted in England. Yet once here, with complete freedom to establish the kind of government and religious freedom they had yearned for in England, they perpetuated the old laws of church-state authority into a new oppression, exchanging one form of persecution for another and jailing those who did not conform. There were frequent whippings for those who dared speak their consciences. For those who disagreed with civil authorities there could be hanging or drowning. Then there was the burning of witches.

Mary Williams delivered her baby and named her "Freeborn." Roger continued to preach vigorously against intolerance, injustice, and all that thwarted the exercise of a free conscience.

The Narraganset Indians befriended him in his exile. Ultimately buying land from them, he was determined to found a colony that was truly free. Twelve men and their families followed Roger Williams to an area that was to become Rhode Island. Pausing one day, in 1636, by a spring of water, they

Spreading to the American Colonies

named the place Providence "because of God's merciful providence to us in our distress." Thanksgiving was offered to God for safety, and a prayer for guidance was made.

Williams was concerned that nowhere in the colonies was baptism practiced solely for believers. Indeed, infant baptism was the usual procedure. Williams could not find such a practice in Scripture and he, himself, had not been baptized after believing in Christ. He wanted to be baptized yet he was the only minister in the group. So, in March of 1639, after concentrated study of the Scriptures, he went to one of his friends, Ezekiel Holliman, who had been in the Salem Church. Telling him of his new convictions, Williams requested that Holliman baptize him. This done, he baptized Holliman and ten others. It can be said that there and then the first Baptist Church in America was formed.

On one of the ships coming into Boston, there arrived a young English doctor, John Clarke. In many ways, he was as disillusioned as Roger Williams had been. He had so abhorred the treatment of a nonconformist woman, Mrs. Ann Hutchinson, that he had joined her family and others in exile. He strongly upheld their rights in matters of conscience and felt compelled to share in their sufferings. Soon he became the leader of the small group which, after wandering and hardship, purchased land from the Indians through Roger Williams' aid where they established what was to be the town of Newport.

THE BAPTIST HERITAGE

They covenanted to be godly people, honoring the Lord Jesus Christ in their lives and with their land. Freedom of conscience was a major concern in their covenant with one another. Thus, the second Baptist Church in America was formed at Newport, Rhode Island.

In July, 1643, Roger Williams sailed for England where certain government policies had shown leniency toward the colonies. Through the help of friends and the blessing of God he obtained a charter that gave the power of self-rule to his colony's towns: Providence, Portsmouth and Newport. This led to the birth of Rhode Island.

The Baptist cause was growing rapidly in New England, as was the new concept and affirmation of believer's baptism, with the rejection of infant baptism. In 1644 the Massachusetts Bay Colony felt it necessary to establish on their law books the illegality of these people they derogatorily termed "the Anabaptists." They called them "troublers of churches," "erroneous persons," "guilty of heresies." They further determined that anyone adhering to and proclaiming their Baptist principles would be banished from the colony.

One notorious incident occurred when Dr. John Clarke, Obadiah Holmes, and John Crandall were invited to Lynn, Massachusetts, to speak to some new converts about their views on baptism and soul freedom. They were summarily arrested. After a brief trial John Clarke was sentenced to a 20-pound

Spreading to the American Colonies

fine or "being well whipt." Obadiah Holmes, a multiple offender, was given a stiffer fine of "thirty pounds or being well whipt." John Crandall was sentenced to "five pounds or being well whipt." Clarke and Crandall paid their fines. Holmes took the whipping. Onlookers who voiced sympathy for the men were immediately arrested and fined. For weeks afterwards Holmes could not rest at night. He tried to sleep fitfully on knees and elbows, so painful was every inch of his body whenever it touched the bed.

By 1651 the Colony of Rhode Island needed a new charter. Together, Roger Williams and Dr. John Clarke sailed to England to negotiate the charter. But it was not until 12 years later (1663) that John Clarke finally miraculously secured the charter from despotic King Charles II. History does not disclose the details of how the charter was secured. Suffice it to say that the charter will always be in the vanguard of state papers dealing with democracy. A portion of that charter reads:

> No person within the said colony, at any time hereafter, shall be anywise molested, punished, disquieted, or called in question for any difference in opinion in matters of religion which do not actually disturb the civil peace of said colony; but that all and every person and persons may from time to time, and at all times thereafter, freely and fully have and enjoy his and their own judgments and consciences in matters of religious commitments.

THE BAPTIST HERITAGE

This charter made its inevitable impact upon American democracy and was one resource for the writing of the First Amendment of the Constitution of the United States. Thus, both Roger Williams and Dr. John Clarke jointly may be called innovators of religious liberty in the United States.

Questions for Thought and Discussion

1. Why do you suppose the Pilgrims and the Puritans formed a Congregational Church in the colonies that was nearly as oppressive as the Anglican Church in England from which they fled?
2. What impresses you the most about Roger Williams? Why?
3. Who should enjoy religious liberty? Do you believe that a Roman Catholic has the right to worship as he pleases? A Buddhist? A member of a Satanist cult? An advocate of Gay Liberation?

Suggestions for Further Study

Torbet, *A History of the Baptists,* pp. 201-208.

4

Expanding the Borders

THE MASSACHUSETTS BAY COLONY'S POLICY toward Baptists was one of banishment, harassment or outright extermination. No permanent organization of Baptist life was allowed until later in the century. So effective had been the persecution that it could be said by 1664 there were no Baptist churches organized in the colonies outside of Providence and the Newport boundaries.

However, by 1665, a Baptist church dared to organize within Boston itself. The pastor, Thomas Goold, and his nine members were under persistent attack by magistrates and citizenry alike. They had all been imprisoned, fined or flogged, at one time or another. So insistent was this persecution that Goold's health failed. These oppressive acts notwithstanding, the church continued to grow until by 1671 its membership stood at 21. During this period

THE BAPTIST HERITAGE

some Quakers had been harried to the gallows and hanged. In England, Parliament had become so incensed by the news that they determined anyone accused of religious crimes in Massachusetts would be sent to England to insure a fair trial. This rebuke to "Bostonian justice" caused the local magistrates to release all religious prisoners and announce to England that they had none to send.

In 1682 a small band of Baptists, some of whom had been members of the Boston church, formed an organization at Kittery, Maine. Driven from Maine a short time later, they migrated to South Carolina where the Charleston church was established around 1684. This was the first Baptist church in the South. Seven years later, in 1691, a fresh wind began to blow for the Baptists in the form of a new charter provided by William and Mary. The charter aligned Massachusetts Bay and Plymouth into one colony and the Baptists were given assurances of toleration. Possessing legal status and certain limited freedoms, the Baptists still had to pay the hated tax for support of a state church. This remained a source of bitterness for them and the cause of much agitation in future days.

At this time, the other great center of Baptist strength besides New England was Philadelphia. By 1688 two churches had been formed there. Within a ten-year span several other churches were organized. In 1707 five churches banned together to form the Philadelphia Baptist Association. The

Expanding the Borders

avowed purpose of this organization was to provide a focus for Baptist concerns, missionary activity, fellowship, and counsel to the churches. No jurisdiction was given to this organization. Strongly Calvinistic[1] in comparison to the Arminian[2] tendencies of the New England churches, the Philadelphia Association heavily influenced the theological direction Baptists in America would take.

Associations had proved their worth among the Baptists of England. Now this new venture in Philadelphia was to become the mainstay of Baptists in early America. Their annual meetings became a kind of clearinghouse for varied theological and social opinions. The churches were not under any compunction to agree with the opinions rendered, but they were given, and they received, the wise views of their brethren. This inevitably had a moderating effect on extremists, as well as providing guidelines where they were desirable.

The Philadelphia Association was so effective in bringing Baptists together for concerted efforts that it became the most influential center of Baptists in

[1] Calvinism: A theological system developed by John Calvin (1509-1564), who predicated his views on the sovereignty of God. It is marked by a doctrine of election or predestination which states that God predetermines or foresees whether a man will or will not be saved.

[2] Arminianism: A theological system developed by Jacobus Arminius (1560-1609) in opposition to the Calvinistic doctrines of irresistible grace and unconditional election. Arminius extolled man's freedom of choice and taught that God knows in advance that man will choose to sin but God does not predestine man to do so.

THE BAPTIST HERITAGE

early America. Because of it, the Charleston Association was formed in South Carolina, followed not many years later by the Warren Association in Rhode Island. Some churches regarded associations as dangerous in that they might acquire authority, as in the local presbyteries, and usurp control over the churches. However, the need for guidance and collective encouragement made associations an important part in Baptist development.

The Philadelphia Association began sending evangelists to remote places. These preachers were not to settle down as pastors, but only to establish churches and then move on to other needy areas of ministry. This evangelistic ardor, this sense of need for taking the Gospel everywhere, has been one of the hallmarks of Baptists throughout their history.

The need for an adequately trained clergy became a priority. The Philadelphia Association began discussions which finally resulted in an academy in New Jersey, a college in Rhode Island (which would become Brown University at a later date), and a theological school in Philadelphia. They even began collecting books and parchments in Philadelphia to form the first substantial library for Baptists. Furthermore, a Confession of Faith was established by this body in 1742 which became a basic document for local church confessions. This confession was Calvinistic in emphasis and set the tone for the future of the Baptist movement in America.

As we have been referring to churches and associ-

Expanding the Borders

ations it might be difficult to grasp the fact that up to the revival known as the Great Awakening (1733) the entire Baptist membership in America did not much exceed 500. These were members of some 47 churches and associations, with 40 in the north and seven south of the Mason-Dixon Line.

During the Great Awakening the Baptists, almost without exception, lacked aggressiveness and enterprise. They remained aloof from the movement and its leaders (Jonathan Edwards, George Whitefield and the Tennents). In some instances, they refused these leaders entry into their churches, even though they would have profited the most from the revival, numerically. The reasons for Baptist indifference will be seen in short order. However, let it be said clearly that one of the most remarkable episodes in American colonial history was the Great Awakening.

It began in Northampton, Massachusetts, in 1733 under the preaching of Jonathan Edwards. It rose to fevered pitch when George Whitefield came to New England for six weeks in 1740. Tremendous crowds were spellbound at the unusual oratory, striking dramatic power, sonorous voice, intense zeal and authentic Evangelical appeal. God's power was evident. Whitefield was reinforced by many others who preached in the open air and traveled far and wide, with spiritual effects upon every village and hamlet. When Whitefield returned to England some of New England's finest preachers such as Jonathan Ed-

THE BAPTIST HERITAGE

wards, Eleazor Wheelock and Joseph Bellamy became, for the time being, itinerant evangelists. In some of their meetings emotional excesses broke out to the discouragement of the evangelists. These excesses harmed their cause with the masses. All in all, the Great Awakening continued to have its good effects for several years with the crest of its power having been passed by 1744. Between the years of 1740 and 1760 church membership was increased by the thousands. Congregationalists and Baptists were most affected by this rapid increase.

The Puritan leaders of New England had very early established the rule that no one could become a member of their churches unless he had had a genuine conversion experience. Before the Great Awakening there had been a general slackening of this rule. Some had argued that conversion was such a personal thing that the matter should be left to the individual and not be judged by the church officials. As long as a moral life was being lived and the church precepts observed, people were presumed to be converted. With the coming of the Great Awakening revivalists there was a resurgence of interest, indeed, an imperative demand for conversion. It was central to the entire movement. "Ye must be born again," was the cry in every town and village. Gilbert Tennent's sermon, "On the Danger of an Unconverted Ministry," was addressed to a careless clergy who had in many instances been so busy fighting political and social battles that they had not

Expanding the Borders

been converted themselves. Whitefield, on one occasion, said:

> The Lord enabled me to open my mouth against unconverted ministers; to caution tutors to take care of their pupils; and also to advise ministers particularly to examine into the experiences of candidates for ordination. For I am verily persuaded the generality of preachers talk of an unknown and unfelt Christ; and the reasons why congregations have been so dead is because they have had dead men preaching to them.

The Baptists were divided over the Great Awakening. There were two parties: the "Regulars" who adhered to the old ways and demeaned revivals; and the "New Lights" or "Separates" who followed the teachings and methods of George Whitefield. A cursory reading of the literature from that time convinces one of the depths at which this controversy was raging.

While many Baptists had opposed the revival movement in New England, Congregationalists of the New Light or Separate mentality came to the conviction that they could find spiritual purity for their churches only as they rejected infant baptism and put the emphasis upon a baptism for believers who had experienced a vital conversion experience. They contended that their churches must separate from the churches of the Standing Order (Episcopalian or Anglican). Soon they had come to the Baptist

THE BAPTIST HERITAGE

position. These former Congregationalists became part of the New Light or Separate Baptists who soon greatly outnumbered the Regulars and eventually were recognized by their Regular Baptist friends. The New Light or Separate Baptists were more evangelistic that the Regulars and more aggressive in seeking civil rights and religious freedom. Under men like Isaac Backus, James Manning and Hezekiah Smith, the Warren Association had been formed, Rhode Island College (Brown University) had come into being, and a relentless attack against the established church had begun.

These New Light or Separate leaders brought a new individualism into American religion. The church as an institution was now secondary, while the individual was primary. He might be an uneducated person from a lower level of society and of meager ability, but none of these mattered. Each person had to stand before God and account for his own soul. Each person could receive direct guidance from the Holy Spirit without the help of a minister. This emphasis upon personal access and commitment to God became the basis of the entire movement. This focus, stereotyped and institutionalized as a part of Baptist beliefs, caused the New Light Baptists to neglect some of the other significant doctrines of the Christian faith. The resulting theological instability caused them to fall into the snares of other movements such as universalism, hyper-Calvinism or hyper-Arminianism. Their

Expanding the Borders

simplistic approach to theology often produced a kind of anti-intellectualism which disparaged an educated ministry. Their refusal to work out the fuller implications of a personal Christian faith in the context of the total Christian tradition and its larger social concerns was to hamper some aspects of the Baptist development. Yet, in spite of these dangers that had developed within the movement, there was a commendable commitment and heroic abandon to winning men to Jesus Christ whatever the cost. God seemed to bless their efforts however simple they might be.

Two very gifted men from the New Light Baptists of Massachusetts settled in Virginia. Shubael Stearns and Daniel Marshall were unusually itinerant, preaching to any audience. Their obvious effectiveness caused the New Light or Separate Baptists to grow rapidly in the south. The original Baptist church in Virginia was known as the Sandy Creek Church, from which came the Sandy Creek Association. Soon there were 42 other Baptist churches in the area and within 20 years some 125 preachers had gone from this center to spread the Gospel. The Sandy Creek Association became a kind of parent body establishing other associations in the south. From the time of the Great Awakening (1733) to the Revolutionary War (1774), some 41 years, the Baptists in America had grown from 500 to 35,000.

There is no question but that the American Revolutionary War (1774-1783) drew the Separate and

Regular Baptists together. Out of their common background and mutual concerns for religious freedom they banned together in concerted action to nullify the Anglican or "Standing Order" institutions. By 1787, Virginia had acquired one unified body of Baptists, and the Anglican Standing Order establishment had become very unpopular throughout the South due to the corruption of its ministers and their careless attitude to the people's desires for religious freedom. The Baptists, by contrast, threw themselves zealously into the revolutionary cause and won the popularity of the masses.

In fairness to history it must be said that the Anglican Standing Order churches of New England were not like their brethren in the South. Indeed, they were in the vanguard of the new burgeoning patriotic movement. Baptists, however, did not grow as rapidly in New England as they did in the South prior to the American Revolutionary War. A partial explanation may be found in that they were seeking redress of grievances at a very strategic, painful time when the New Englanders were seeking to thwart English tyranny. The Baptists attempted to use the sensitive situation to their own ends by forcing their demands for religious liberty, cessation of taxes for state churches, and the like; they threatened to withhold cooperation in the revolutionary efforts and to present an appeal to Britain for the rights denied them by colonial magistrates. Understandably they were unpopular in New England. It needs

Expanding the Borders

to be said, however, that once the Revolutionary War began the Baptists were patriotically at the forefront even though their name had been clouded by their aggressive insensitivity.

As the year 1800 dawned, there were fewer Baptists in the New England States of Massachusetts, Connecticut, Rhode Island and New Hampshire combined than in the State of Virginia. Also, the combined Baptists of New York, Pennsylvania, New Jersey and Delaware did not much surpass that of North Carolina. At this point in time America had about 100,000 Baptists. The rapid expansion of the movement can be seen more clearly when we remember that at the beginning of the Great Awakening (1733) there were not more than 500 Baptists in America; at the beginning of the Revolutionary War (1774) there were 35,000; then just 26 years later, at the turn of the century (1800), there were 100,000. These figures reveal something of the amazing growth pattern.

With the arrival of civil liberty following the Revolutionary War, there was not yet any guarantee of religious liberty. But this was soon to follow. New York established a new constitution in 1777 which permitted "the free exercise of religious profession and worship without discrimination or preference." In 1785 Thomas Jefferson drew up a constitutional provision allowing religious freedom in Virginia. His friend James Madison strongly supported this provision. As the other colonies assumed statehood they created provisions in their constitutions that provided guarantees for religious freedom. The culmination of all these efforts was in the Federal Constitution's First Amendment (1789) providing that "Congress shall make no law respecting an establishment of religion, or prohibiting the free exercise thereof."

Finally, in 1833, Massachusetts adopted a constitution which provided a thorough-going religious liberty. From then on, every state in America would give itself to the guarantee of religious liberty, and separation of church and state.

With the opening of the trans-Appalachian frontier Baptists discovered their greatest opportunity. Their spiritual dynamic and their farmer preachers were especially adapted to the needs of the West. It was precisely the success of these dauntless Baptists in meeting the religious needs of the frontier that made them one of the great denominations of America.

Questions for Thought and Discussion

1. What are some of the advantages of associations of churches in comparison to independent churches? What disadvantages are there?
2. It may sometimes seem that the difference between Calvinism and Arminianism is only theoretical. What actual difference in life-style is evident in Baptist history?

Expanding the Borders

3. How can an individual or a church determine whether or not a person has been truly "converted" or "born again"?

4. Who should have the responsibility for determining this matter—the church, each individual, no one but God? Why?

5. How do some of the major problems and effects of the Great Awakening compare with similar situations in contemporary revivals or evangelistic campaigns?

6. Why would the new individualism introduced into American religion during the time of the Great Awakening sometimes lead to theological error?

7. What do you believe accounts for the fact that Baptists grew from only 500 members in 1733 to about 100,000 in 1800?

Suggestions for Further Study

1. Robert T. Handy, "The Philadelphia Tradition," *Baptist Concepts of the Church,* ed. Winthrop S. Hudson, op. cit., pp. 30-52.

2. Torbet, *A History of the Baptists,* pp. 208-234.

5

Into All the World

SO MANY CONVERTS WERE COMING into the Baptist ranks that by 1812 there were 172,972 Baptists in America. The South had 114,545 while New England had 32,272 and the Middle States 26,155. Most of this growth resulted from the preaching and the commitment of illiterate evangelists, a plucky lot, with a deep faith in Jesus Christ as Savior and Lord.

Many Europeans had heard about this "new land of opportunity." Bored with their plight in the old country's static society, many thousands began what was at first a trickle and then a mighty river of migration. For the local settlers on the Atlantic seaboard it was commonplace to see myriads of new people landing from ships to pause briefly and then be off for "the West." Indeed, their own neighbors, friends and relatives would suddenly pile belongings

Into All the World

high on their wagons and set out to find their new world of hope and challenge.

At this point in our story we must pause and pick up a strand of significant history back in England which was to have far-reaching effects upon these pioneers. William Carey was the humble pastor of a Baptist church in Moulton, England, in 1787. He received a salary of only $75 a year. Because of the poverty of his church members he worked as a cobbler. While he worked he would also study books. He had a gift for languages and learned five, including Greek and Hebrew, within seven years. He also borrowed books of history and geography. One about Captain Cook's voyages particularly impressed him. This turned his mind to the world, and the lost people on the various continents.

It is said that in a Baptist gathering Carey once stood to plead for a mission to the heathen and an older pastor in the audience said: "Sit down, young man; when the Lord gets ready to convert the heathen he will do it without your help or mine!" But Carey never backed away from the overwhelming challenge of a world needing Jesus Christ.

Because of his interest in missions and his obvious ability he was asked to speak at his association in Nottingham on May 30, 1792. His text was Isaiah 44:2, 3, and his outline, "Expect great things from God; attempt great things for God." That message marked a turning point in Baptist history. Everyone who heard it was aroused to their newly understood responsibility for the lost heathen of the world. A resolution was passed that would allow for the establishment of the English Baptist Missionary Society on October 2, 1792 in Kettering, England. The total contribution that day to the first treasury of the Society was 13 pounds, two shillings and six pence. Not much to start with, but what a beginning! This Mission Society finally had sufficient funds to send William Carey and Dr. John Thomas, a physician, to India where they labored for seven years before seeing their first convert.

Soon, many were receiving Christ as their Savior and being baptized. Carey translated the Scriptures into their language as well as writing dictionaries, grammars and the like. Indeed, it is said that prior to Carey's death he had translated or supervised the translation of the Scriptures into 40 languages or dialects. He surely was the "Father of the Missionary movement" that all Christians know today.

Word of these exciting happenings in India came to New England, and it was not long before Americans were enthusiastic about foreign missions. People would read of the exploits of Carey and his associates and begin to ask themselves whether or not God wanted them to go overseas with the Gospel. Young American men and women began to commit themselves to missionary service.

Adoniram Judson, son of the pastor of the Plymouth Congregational Church, heard God's call. Contrary to his parents' pleadings he decided to go into foreign missionary service. On February 19, 1812, the ship *Caravan* sailed out of Salem harbor on its way to Calcutta, India, with America's first foreign missionaries, Ann and Adoniram Judson, and Samuel and Harriet Newell.

Aboard ship they had ample time to study the Scriptures. Since they would be associated with Baptists in India, they decided they ought to know more about the teachings of Scripture about infant baptism. The more they studied the less assured they were of their own position favoring infant baptism. They decided that they had to seek immersion and become Baptists even though this would be exceedingly embarrassing for the newly organized Congregational Mission Board back home which was supporting them. One of their first requests upon arriving was to be immersed in the Baptist Chapel at Calcutta.

Carey evidently encouraged the Judsons to go to Rangoon, Burma, which they did. There the Judsons, now fervent Baptists, shared the Gospel of Jesus Christ with all those with whom they came into contact. Despite threats, beatings, imprisonment, torture, and even the eventual death of his wife, Ann, Adoniram Judson continued preaching, translating and living out the love of Jesus Christ. He opened schools for the Burmese to study the Scriptures and train native evangelists. His ministry extended to the Karen hill tribes who eagerly responded to the Gospel, and are even today one of the

THE BAPTIST HERITAGE

most rapidly growing groups of Christians in the world.

Luther Rice, who had been sent by the same Mission Society from New England to India, though on a different ship than the Judsons, had had a similar experience. He, too, had come to some new conclusions about baptism prior to meeting William Carey in India, and he also was brought into the Baptist family through immersion. Rice felt he should not remain in India, but rather come back to America to tell the story of missions, thereby helping to raise necessary funds for the work in India.

He traveled tirelessly from Maine to Georgia as one of God's most effective voices for the missionary cause. In fact, he was so effective that he was instrumental in bringing about the assembly of 33 delegates from 11 states at Philadelphia, in 1814, to form a General Convention of American Baptists. Because of scheduled meetings every three years, it became known as the Triennial Convention. Within a few years several affiliated societies arose out of this organization: the American Baptist Publication Society in 1824; the American Baptist Home Mission Society in 1832; and the American and Foreign Bible Society in 1837. These societies were the organizations that bound the churches together in their General Convention.

John Mason Peck was commissioned by the Triennial Convention in 1817 as their missionary to the region west of the Mississippi. He packed up his little family and in great faith took on weather, pitfalls and the dangers of traveling some 1,200 miles to a primitive land.

He was constantly on the move, traveling over 3,500 miles on horseback or by foot in one year's time. On several occasions he became lost in the wilderness. He was frequently drenched by rains, and for days lived in cold damp clothing. At times he was seriously ill. He was endangered by thieves or marauders yet he constantly put his trust in his Lord. The perils of cold, hunger, weariness, Indians, rivers, and storms could not dissuade him. He reminds us of the description of the apostle Paul in II Corinthians 11:26-29 (Phillips):

> In my travels I have been in constant danger from rivers, from bandits, from my own countrymen, and from pagans. I have faced danger in city streets, danger in the desert, danger on the high seas, danger among false Christians. I have known exhaustion, many sleepless nights, hunger and thirst, fasting, cold and exposure. Apart from all external trials I have the daily burden of responsibility for all the churches.

When Peck was 28 years of age, at the beginning of his great ministry, he entered the following words into his diary: "I have now put my hands to the plow. O Lord, may I never turn back—never regret this step. It is my duty to live, to labor, to die as a kind of pioneer in advancing the Gospel." This he did.

THE BAPTIST HERITAGE

Peck was as much a missionary as was Judson or Carey. Within three years after arriving at St. Louis he had established 50 schools, several churches, encouraged a plan for itinerant ministers, planned for a college, and inaugurated a ministry among the Indians. He was being increasingly maligned by a group of anti-mission Baptists centered in Kentucky who had moved into other western territories. They felt it was "sacreligious to attempt to lead men to conversion" since their hyper-Calvinistic theology told them that "God already knew who would be saved and who would be damned." "Missions were unnecessary at least and presumptious before God, at most." So loud and clamorous were the cries of the hyper-Calvinists that the Triennial Convention shamefully allowed itself to withdraw its support from this mission frontier—partly because of low funds, and partly to keep peace. The work struggled for a while until the Massachusetts Baptists sent their representative, Elder Jonathan Going, to survey Peck's work for several months. Going and Peck traveled together until Elder Going saw the validity of Peck's work. They drew up a mutual plan for what was to be known as the American Baptist Home Mission Society. On April 27, 1832, the new society was formed in New York and missionary work at home and on the frontier was continued at a stepped-up pace.

Our Baptist heritage lifts high four great representative names—Carey, Judson, Rice and Peck. They

Into All the World

stand for hosts of other outstanding and committed men and women who were used by the Holy Spirit in the Baptist movement's rapid growth in frontier America.

In spite of this quality of leadership, the pressures of a burgeoning population were making themselves felt in our nation. Regional and cultural differences were taking shape. Theological fractures were showing up. Indeed, at this time Baptists could be said to be divided into two distinct camps—missionary Baptists and anti-missionary Baptists. We thank God today that the missionary emphasis won out, and the anti-missionary concept virtually died.

At the Triennial meeting in 1817, a foreboding event took place, a warning of events to come, and one that would ultimately split the Baptists of America. A significant disagreement arose between two groups, the northern and the southern churches, over the expansion of the Convention's authority. Some delegates desired greater central control over all missionary and evangelistic activity while others pressed for separate control of each affiliated society or organization. The "separate control" concept, advocated by the north, won the day. As a result of this decision some of the major Baptist societies were formed, such as the American Baptist Home Missions Society and the American Baptist Publication Society.

However, a breach had been made that shaped up along geographical lines. The southern contingent of representatives were not for central authority in the sense of one central church. Rather they sincerely felt that the cooperative activities of all the disparate groups involved in education, evangelism and missions could better be carried on and financed without duplication of effort if they were coordinated by a central planning organization. That organization, as the southern churches saw it, would be accountable to the individual churches, and would have no authority except that which was voted it by the various affiliated churches.

However, the northern churches' concept of the individuality and autonomy of the societies, as we have seen, won in the final tally. An additional aggravation to the southern churches was that the location of the offices of these respective societies were kept in the northern cities of Boston, New York and Philadelphia.

In addition, serious feelings were developing around the issue of slavery. It must be said that slavery was not brought up as a divisive issue prior to 1830. Indeed, Baptists in Virginia in 1789 called upon their legislators to abolish slavery gradually. Nothing was done by the legislature, however. Because of the sensitivity of the issue most Baptists in the southern states chose to skirt the matter and not make it a divisive issue in view of the fact that some of the churches had large numbers of people within their memberships who were slaveholders. The matter was left to the individual conscience.

Into All the World

When the General Convention met at Philadelphia in 1844 there were those who made every effort to avoid a confrontation over slavery. The southern delegations, however, did not seem to share this feeling. Shortly after this meeting the Georgia Baptist Convention instructed its leaders to present the Rev. James Reeves as a missionary to the Cherokee Indians. Since Reeves was a slaveholder, this seemed to be a deliberate test case. The nomination was rejected by a seven to five vote.

To further aggravate matters the Home Mission Board was scored publicly by the Alabama Convention when the board retired Rev. Jesse Bushyhead, who was well liked and quite effective among the Indians, on the grounds that he owned slaves. The battle lines were quickly drawn.

The Virginia Baptist Foreign Mission Society called for a convening of southern churches in Augusta, Georgia. Three hundred delegates came in response to the call, and in May of 1845 the organization of the Southern Baptist Convention took place. A section from the resolution of this first meeting states:

> Northern and Southern Baptists are still brethren. They differ in no article of faith. They are guided by the same principle of gospel order. . . We do not regard the rupture as extending to foundation principles, nor can we think that the great body of our northern brethren will so regard it.

But the break was clean and remains to this day.

THE BAPTIST HERITAGE

The northern Baptists, asserting their autonomy in their local churches and societies, were much slower in bringing their churches together into a single national body. But it was inevitable, as the nation expanded and greater distances separated Baptists from one another, that a tighter organizational structure was needed in the north to properly promote communication and missionary interests. Thus, the Northern Baptist Convention was organized in Washington, D.C., on May 16, 1907, with Charles Evans Hughes as its first President. The name was changed in 1950 to the American Baptist Convention. In 1973 a further name change was made to the "American Baptist Churches of the U.S.A."

Meanwhile, other Baptist denominations have come into being. Some were originally formed because of ethnic ties, though this may or may not be a significant factor in their character today. For example, the Baptist General Conference was originally a Swedish group, the Free Will Baptists have a Welsh background, and the National Primitive Baptist Convention of the U.S.A. is a black organization.

Some denominations arose through questions of government and policy. The National Baptist Convention of America, a black denomination formed in 1895, later separated into two groups, one keeping the original name, the other calling itself the National Baptist Convention of the U.S.A., Inc. This group in turn spawned the Progressive National Baptist Convention, Inc., in 1961.

Into All the World

Other bodies have been formed when doctrinal issues and matters of polity were disputed. The General Association of Regular Baptist Churches was formed in 1932 when 22 churches left the American Baptist Convention in protest over what they considered to be modernist tendencies and the denial of historic Baptist principles. The Conservative Baptist Association of America also developed out of a doctrinal disagreement with the American Baptist Convention.

Following to the logical end their love of freedom and independence, various other Baptist groups have established themselves throughout the United States and Canada. In spite of disagreement on minor details, they have developed a recognizble identity as Baptists, and, in doing so, have contributed to the spiritual life of the world.

On July 11-18, 1905, Baptists from all over the world responded to an invitation from British leaders to meet in London for a Baptist world convention. Some 23 nations responded with delegates. They organized what has been known since as the Baptist World Alliance whose constitution assuringly said: "The Alliance may in no way interfere with the independence of the churches or assume administrative functions of existing organizations."

Unless prevented by war or other circumstances, the Alliance has convened in some major city in the world every five years. It functions as an agency of communication between Baptists through publications, films, radio, television, personal visits, and correspondence. It is also a forum for study and fraternal discussion of doctrines, practices, and ways of witness to the world. It is a channel of cooperation in extending help to each other and to those in need. It is on constant guard for religious rights of people in all lands. Its world relief activities are perhaps some of the most significant as it provides tons of food and clothing for the destitute in the name of Christ. One never-to-be forgotten highlight of every congress program is the roll call of nations, when nationals of every country represented at the meeting are presented to tell the story of Baptist work in their lands.

At present, some 129 countries of the world have Baptist work within their borders. Their fellowship encompasses over 32 million baptized believers. In Egypt, Spain, Ceylon and scores of other countries, minority groups of Baptists bear courageous witness to their faith under great difficulties. Far back in the hills of Assam, near the Chinese border, there are 3,000 Baptist churches with a baptized membership of about 280,000. In recent times, from that field alone, some 15,000 men and women have accepted Jesus Christ as Lord and Savior each year. In the highlands of New Guinea savages have been won to Christ. Russia has an estimated 5,400 Baptist churches filled to overflowing several times weekly as people meet eagerly and hungrily for Bible study and worship. In the U.S.A., Baptists affiliated in

Into All the World

some 29 different conventions and associations constitute the fastest growing major denomination in Christendom.

The key to this growth is that Baptists have been historically evangelistic, passionately missionary, studiously about the work of Christian education, and fully involved in the brokenness and misery of human life. They have felt the heartbeat of the Savior who loved the world so much that He became a man in order to carry our griefs and sorrows. They have understood that He took our brokenness upon Himself and loved us through death and beyond. And they have clearly seen that, compared with His sacrifice, all the missionary endeavor, all the ministry, all the social action, all of man's best efforts are feeble expressions of His own love. But they have also seen that these expressions are the only adequate outward signs of the inward response of faith. And the Lord has blessed that faith.

Questions for Thought and Discussion

1. What are the essential characteristics of a missionary as seen in men such as William Carey and Adoniram Judson? In what ways do modern missionaries differ, if at all?
2. What are the differences between foreign missions as seen in the work of Carey and Judson and the home missions work of John Peck on the frontier of the United States?

THE BAPTIST HERITAGE

3. How would you answer the arguments against missions that were raised by the hyper-Calvinists?
4. What major disagreements accounted for the split between the Baptists of the North and those of the South?
5. What do you believe, historically, to be the single most compelling motive behind Baptist missions? Is that motive valid today? Why or why not?

Suggestions for Further Study

Torbet, *A History of the Baptists,* pp. 243-253, 261-263, and 282-297.

PART II: Beliefs

6

The People of a Book

A CHILD WITH POOR VISION once visited a lion's cage at the local zoo. She screwed up her face and squinted to see whatever was inside the cage. Having never seen a lion before, she did not know what to expect. Her weak eyes searched the unclear objects, but she could see only a hairy tail hanging down through the bars. "I thought the lion would be different," she said, "but it looks like a yellow rope."

Just so, there are Baptists who have discovered only the tail end of our Baptist distinctives and, tragically, they have become as narrow as the tail they devoutly believe in. It is possible to be a Baptist and build one's faith around unimportant or secondary issues. We need to remind ourselves that while we hold to distinctive beliefs that might differ significantly from other Christian groups, the fundamentals of our faith are affirmed by most Christians the world over. These common doctrines should be emphasized in our friendships with others. Our time should not be devoted to secondary issues that may be divisive.

Unlike many historic Christian bodies, Baptists do not derive their beliefs from councils or ecclesiastical bodies of any name, directly or indirectly. Because of dogged adherence to the Bible as our sole authority for faith and practice we have been known as "people of the Book." The Reformers shouted, "sola Scriptura, sola fide" (which means "only the Scriptures provide the basis for our faith"; and, "our salvation comes solely by faith in Jesus Christ"). These affirmations became the platform for later Baptists.

There are at least three voices that have confirmed and attested the Scripture's authenticity and inspiration. First, there is the *voice of the Bible itself,* speaking clearly on its own behalf. For example, one cannot read the Old Testament without seeing that it is God, not man, who is speaking. Some 2,600 times in the Old Testament one finds such statements as "Thus saith the Lord. . ."; "The word of the Lord came unto me saying. . ."; "The Lord God called unto Adam and said. . ."; "God spake unto Israel . . ."; or "These are the words which the Lord hath commanded. . . ."

The apostle Paul affirmed "All scripture is given by inspiration of God," that is, it is literally "God-breathed" (II Tim. 3:16). The apostle Peter ex-

The People of a Book

pounded the same theme when he asserted, "holy men of God spake as they were moved by the Holy Ghost" (II Pet. 1:21). Most significantly, our Lord Himself emphasized that He had not come to destroy the law and the prophets but to fulfill them. Then He added, "One jot or one tittle shall in no wise pass... till all be fulfilled" (Mt. 5:18), thus revealing a lofty and thorough espousal of the Scriptures as the trustworthy Word of God. Indeed, when Jesus was tempted in the wilderness by Satan, Matthew reminds us of His use of Scripture to repulse the Enemy. He responded to each temptation with the words: "It is written..." (Mt. 4: 4, 7, 10)—the bold implication being that it is the use of the absolute, authoritative Word of God that foils Satan's destructive plan. Our Lord's teaching emphatically substantiates the Scriptures as God's message to mankind.

As the Old Testament affirms the voice of the one who *will* come to mankind, so the New Testament speaks of the one who *has* come. It sings the Good News, the Gospel, that He who was in their midst was, by His preaching and ministry, the Word of God "in the flesh."

A second voice gives testimony to the Word of God; it is the *voice of history*. The long years of total acceptance of the authoritative place of the Bible in the life of the Church is one of the finest arguments for the divine inspiration of the Bible. In addition to the fixed Old Testament canon, only those New Testament books were accepted that had the ap-

THE BAPTIST HERITAGE

proval of, or originated with the apostles. The Church Fathers, who led the churches during the few hundred years immediately following Christ's ascension and the era of the apostles, differed in many ways. However, one thing they all virtually agreed upon was the inspired Word of God. They did not consider their own writings as inspired or on par with the Word of God. The same attitude prevailed among the Reformers of the 1500's, and the Anabaptists of Europe, and the Puritans and Separatists of England.

Despite all the tortures, burnings or hangings of people who placed the Bible over any other authority, the radical transformation which the reception of its message produced in their lives caused them to continue in their tenacity. When persecution came "the blood of the martyrs became the seed of the church." Some books inform, some reform, but the Bible transforms. History has borne overwhelming testimony to this fact.

It was Voltaire, the French skeptic (1694-1778 A.D.) who claimed that in one hundred years the Bible would be a forgotten book. It was not long thereafter, following Voltaire's death, that the very building in which he wrote housed a printing press that published more Bibles annually than Voltaire's books would sell in a lifetime.

For all flesh is as grass, and all the glory of man as the flower of grass. The grass withereth, and the flower thereof falleth away: But the word of the Lord endureth for ever. And this is the word which by the gospel is preached unto you (I Pet. 1: 24, 25).

A third voice affirming the authority and inspiration of Scripture is that of *God Himself*. The first voice, that of Scripture, and the second, that of history, are impressive. But this voice, this testimony, is overwhelmingly impressive. For it says: "If the Bible is indeed God's inspired Word, it must always be self-authenticating; it doesn't need man's sanction and approval." Here is God the Spirit, Himself, testifying to the truth of His Word, the Bible. As its source and inspiration, He authenticates it to the heart of every person who believes on Him. The Holy Spirit convicts, convinces and confirms us in the fact that our assurance of salvation is based on no other source of authority than the self-authenticating Word of God. It is by the inner witness of the Holy Spirit that we understand and apply to our own lives the Biblical message. God's Spirit opens the eye of faith to know, internally, that "all Scripture is inspired of God."

Some Christians have said that the Bible "contains" the Word of God. Others have said that the Bible "becomes" the Word of God, subjectively, when you read it in faith. Both propositions are true, but still more needs to be said. The Bible contains the Word of God because all of it *is* His Word. It becomes the Word to us, subjectively, as the Holy

THE BAPTIST HERITAGE

Spirit does His work in our minds and hearts. But it becomes the Word only because it *is* the Word in the first place.

While the voice of God's Holy Spirit to us is both subjective and objective, it is also unimpeachable and inerrant, and cannot be contradicted. He who feels he can contradict this witness of God has not received that witness in the first place.

To the intellectually honest person who claims he has not yet heard this witness of the Spirit regarding the Bible, we can only suggest that he has, perhaps, inadvertently removed himself by unbelief or cynicism from the only context in which he can know God's truth about the Scriptures.

> But the man who isn't a Christian can't understand and can't accept these thoughts from God, which the Holy Spirit teaches us. They sound foolish to him, because only those who have the Holy Spirit within them can understand what the Holy Spirit means. Others just can't take it in (I Cor. 2:14, The Living Bible).

President Abraham Lincoln seemed to confirm the point that God's voice is heard in the Scriptures in a self-authenticating manner, when he said:

> The character of the Bible is easily established, at least to my satisfaction. It is the only book that claims to be God's book. It describes a Governor omnipotent enough to operate this great machine

The People of a Book

and declares that he made it. It states other facts that we cannot comprehend. What shall we do with them? Now let us treat the Bible fairly. If we had a witness on the stand whose general story we knew was true, we would believe him when he asserted facts of which we had no evidence. We ought to treat the Bible with equal fairness. I decided a long time ago that it was less difficult to believe that the Bible was what it claimed to be than to disbelieve it. This great Book of God is the best gift which God ever has given to man.

To summarize, Baptists have believed, down through the years, that the Bible is the Word of God, authored by God but written down as holy men were "inbreathed" or inspired to write. Some 40 persons from varied positions in life were involved. Some of them were sheepherders, others were fishermen. One was a medical doctor. Another was a tax collector. Some were well educated and others had no formal education at all. As God breathed His message into their hearts and minds they took their pens and wrote, employing their own styles and personalities, with all of their own linguistic individuality. The amazing harmony that came out of the writings of these 40 men, over a 1,500-year span, can be understood only if we see God as its one and only Author. The Bible can be called truly a miracle of God's own handiwork.

While Baptists have always affirmed the inspiration of the Holy Scriptures, they have not believed

THE BAPTIST HERITAGE

that every portion of the Bible had equal importance. In other words, one could not responsibly say that Leviticus, Chapter 3, is equal in importance to John, Chapter 3. Many other examples could be cited to show that while the Bible is equally inspired, its portions are not necessarily of equal relevance.

However, every part of the Bible has a purpose. It is to reveal God's dealings with the world, His saving acts. So one might call Bible history "the history of salvation"; Bible music "the music of salvation"; Bible chronology "the chronology of salvation"; Biblical theology "the theology of salvation."

In the words of the New Hampshire Confession of Faith (1833):

> We believe that the Holy Bible was written by men divinely inspired and is a perfect treasure of heavenly instruction; that it has God for its author, salvation for its end, and truth without any mixture of error for its matter; and it reveals the principles by which God will judge us; and therefore is, and shall remain to the end of the world, the true center of Christian union, and the supreme standard by which all human conduct, creeds, and opinions should be tried.

The apostle Paul reminded Timothy that the Scriptures would make him "wise unto salvation through faith which is in Christ Jesus" (II Tim. 3:15). Peter enjoins his audience to remember that "the word of the Lord endureth for ever" (I Pet. 1:25). John the beloved, writing what may well be the last of all the Biblical writings, says: "These are written that you may believe that Jesus is the Christ, the Son of God, and that believing you may have life in his name" (Jn. 20:31, RSV).

Questions for Thought and Discussion

1. What is unique about the Bible's claim to be "God-breathed"? There are, after all, other religious books written by "holy" men.
2. Why is it important to affirm the inspiration and authority of Scripture?
3. What is the difference between saying that the Bible "contains the Word of God" and saying that it "becomes the Word of God when you read it in faith"? How do these two definitions differ from the statement that the Bible "is the Word of God"?
4. What do you think of the author's point that it is not necessary to regard every portion of the Bible as equally important?
5. What criteria do you use for deciding the relative importance of a portion of Scripture?

7

A Gospel That Changes Persons

THE HISTORY OF THE BAPTISTS, as we have seen, shows their deep involvement in political and civil struggles for freedom of conscience in England, in the continent, and later in the American colonies. The Baptists also manifested a graciousness and respect to people of all classes, with a particular care and sympathy for the downtrodden. From this we might assume that these Baptists were merely benevolent activists who were busily engaged with many peripheral facets of the Christian faith, yet missing the core of the Gospel, the concern for individual salvation. However, this was not true. Their willingness to work with all kinds of people across organizational lines, their concern for the disenfranchised and broken hearted—these were but manifestations of a deeper commitment to the person and work of Jesus Christ.

A Gospel That Changes Persons

One senses this cause-and-effect relationship in one of John Smyth's last statements, written a few months prior to his death, in his book *Retraction and Confirmation* (1612). He retracted nothing he had said, substantively, over the years of his ministry. What he did retract was the spirit of censure in which many of his judgments had been made against others. "I protest," he said, "against that my former course of censuringe other persons, and especially for all those hard phrases, wherwith I have in any of my writings, inveighed against either England or the seperation." This spirit, he admitted, "hath broken the rules of love and charitie, which is the superiour law." Then he accented his beliefs as follows:

> The Articles of Religion which are the ground of my salvation are these, wherein I differ from no good Christian: That Jesus Christ, the Son of God and the Son of Mary, is the anointed King, Priest and Prophet of the Church, the only Mediator of the New Testament, and that through repentance and faith in Him Who alone is our Savior we receive remission of sins and the Holy Ghost in this life, and therewith all the redemption of our bodies and everlasting life in the resurrection of the body. And whosoever walketh according to this rule, I must needs acknowledge him as my brother; yea, although he differ from me in divers other particulars.

The great hearts, both within and without the Baptist family, have clearly delineated for us the necessity of repentance and faith. But these terms sound theological and difficult. There seem to be built-in assumptions in such words. Let us attempt to clarify. Repentance always relates to that *from which* I turn, and faith to that *toward which* I turn. They are closely related but different. I turn from my sin, with godly sorrow over the sin, and turn toward God with faith-filled expectation that He will forgive, cleanse, and restore whatever has been broken by my alienation.

Now this presupposes a very important concept, "sin." Newspapers and newscasts give evidence of human sin—hate, lust, greed, prejudice, manipulation—in a thousand different ways. Each time we see a policeman, a soldier, or even a schoolroom filled with children we should know that something has gone wrong somewhere back at the beginning. If humans were assured of inevitable perfection and bliss, every little child would automatically progress in growth and morality. The evidence is to the contrary, however. Every child needs to know the parameters of life, the ground-rules of the game, and have a teacher to "hem" him in for his own sake. There is a propensity within each child to "take over," to "rule or ruin," to "have his own way." Every classroom reminds us that "Johnny" must learn to raise his hand, take his turn, do his assignments, obey the rules. Schools are needed not only to convey a great body of information and skills that make for harmonious participation in life, but to

A Gospel That Changes Persons

help form a sense of responsibility as well. For we are not born with a sense of responsibility, with a desire to share, or with a benevolent spirit. We seek simply to obtain pleasure and avoid pain.

Ironically, in all human pleasure-seeking and pain-avoidance we usually end up functionally attempting to be our own god with the resultant inevitable misery which we bring upon ourselves and our society. We assiduously avoid and evade God. This is the heart of our sin-problem: a horrendous ego, an obsession with our own ability to extricate ourselves from any situation and ultimately succeed, an incurable optimism about our condition. Frantically sensing our own insecurity deep within, we intuitively know we are broken and fragmented apart from God. We know, in our most honest moments, that we have not gotten it all together. We are Humpty-Dumpty who has fallen from the wall, and we are broken beyond our power to repair.

Seneca said: "Men love their vices and hate them at the same time." He was accenting the strange paradox that sin has produced within mankind. The gangster helps his widowed mother with gentle tenderness an hour before strangling a victim. A rapist goes home and counsels his little sister about the dangers of dark streets at night. A prostitute takes on the support of a little orphan with motherly tenderness.

On the one hand we have futility, degradation and evil. On the other are goodness, kindness, gentleness and love. This paradox, this bifurcation of life, confirms man's essential illness. Though created in God's image, he is sick unto death with the disease of sinfulness, of being contrary to the will and law of God. One does not have to be a gangster or a rapist or a prostitute to discover a contrary heart and a fragmented nature.

Someone says, "I go to church, and I try to be good, and I believe in God. Doesn't that make me a Christian?" Not so! A cat may have kittens in an old oven, but that doesn't make them biscuits! Because one goes into a garage one does not become an automobile. Just so, church attendance, good deeds, and mental assent to the existence of a God do not make someone a Christian. A person might go to church to evade God.

How? Well it is ironically simple. It is one thing to be an out-and-out evil person. It is another thing to go to church and go through the motions of piety—to cover up, to soothe the conscience, to put up a facade to hide the real state of the heart and mind. In this way, churchgoing and good deeds contribute to hypocrisy, deception and godlessness. Playing at religion is a game that most of us learn very early in life.

Should church attendance be omitted then? Certainly not. The church is a good place for sinners and saints if they are aware of their need and are honestly seeking to find forgiveness and the strength of God in worship. But we need to recognize and confess

A Gospel That Changes Persons

our motives. Otherwise, church can become a farce.

Where then did evil come from? God made a complete world with perfect surroundings, and there was to be no sickness or death in it. He gave perfect man the order to take charge of the world and use it to the glory of God. But there was one thing man was not to do:

> And the Lord God commanded the man, saying, Of every tree of the garden thou mayest freely eat: But of the tree of the knowledge of good and evil, thou shalt not eat of it: for in the day that thou eatest thereof thou shalt surely die (Gen. 2:16, 17).

Man disobeyed and death has worked in mind and heart and soul ever since.

If God knew man would disobey and eat the fruit, why did God allow it? He had given man every reason not to disobey in the very abundance and goodness of the Garden. But, because there is no love without choice, God had to give man an alternative in order to create the possibility of a reciprocal, spontaneous love. If God had loaded the situation, making it impossible for man to choose anything other than His own will, He would have precluded the possibility of real love between man and Himself. So, God, because He desired a vital, real, love-commitment from His children, gave them a vital option—even if their wrong choice brought havoc.

THE BAPTIST HERITAGE

Sin, the old Baptist divines discovered as they searched the Scriptures, was revolt against God. It was the establishment of a false independence. In the Garden man could choose to serve God—or rebel and seek to build his own world without God. The whole idea behind the tree of knowledge of good and evil was a test.

The immediate cause of man's sin was "the lust of the flesh, and the lust of the eyes, and the pride of life" (I Jn. 2:16).

> And when the woman saw that the tree was good for food, and that it was pleasant to the eyes, and a tree to be desired to make one wise, she took of the fruit thereof, and did eat, and gave also unto her husband with her; and he did eat (Gen. 3:6).

The result of disobedience was death in all its forms: physical, spiritual, moral, economic, political. Had Adam and Eve obeyed God, we can hardly imagine what fantastic possibilities man would have enjoyed in the thousands of years that have passed since then. There would have been no lust, hatred, wars, disease, prejudice, poverty or hunger. God and man together would have built on this planet a glorious social order that would have been unbelievably meaningful and enjoyable.

In 1792, William Carey, the famous Baptist missionary, wrote a pamphlet entitled "An Enquiry into the Obligations of Christians" which had much to do

A Gospel That Changes Persons

with the formation of the First Baptist Missionary Society in England. In this pamphlet he said:

> Sin was introduced amongst the children of men by the fall of Adam and has ever since been spreading its baneful influence. By changing its appearances to suit the circumstances of the times, it has grown up in ten thousand forms, and constantly counteracted the will and designs of God. . . . Yet God repeatedly made known his intention to prevail finally over all the power of the Devil, and to destroy all his works, and set up his own kingdom and interest among men, and extend it as universally as Satan had extended his. It was just for this purpose that the Messiah came and died, that God might be just, and the justifier of all that should believe in him.

Sin, then, is the culprit denounced by the Scriptures. The New Testament verb for "sin" means, literally, "to miss the target." Sin is the missing of the target, the standard, which God has established for our lives. Thus, sin is our failure and inability to live up to God's requirements. "All we like sheep have gone astray" (Isa. 53:6).

Now, this sinfulness is not something we can blame solely on Adam. He passed on to us the tendency to sin but we are sinners by personal choice. Because we choose ourselves rather than God, sin brings disastrous results to our lives. *The mind* is affected. A person may be brilliant in various intellectual pursuits, but the Bible says he is unable to think correctly. He cannot comprehend the things of God no matter how brilliant he may be. Prior to conversion to Jesus Christ, the Holy Spirit of God must bring enlightenment to the human mind or there is no possibility of genuine repentance and conversion. The Gospel does not demean the mind, but it stresses the lordship of Jesus Christ over it.

Likewise, the Bible states that the *emotions* are warped by the disease of sin. We not only think inadequately but we emote wrongly. We often love wrong things and despise many of the right things. Our emotional life needs to be overhauled by Jesus Christ or else we will go amuck at the feeling-levels of life. Since we are guided more by emotion than reason, one can readily see the danger of an unconverted set of emotions.

The Bible points to the effects of sin on *the will*. Jesus said: "Whosoever committeth sin is the servant of sin" (Jn. 8: 34). Vast numbers live under the control of pride, jealousy, and hatreds even as others live under the control of drugs, pleasure-seeking or money. They have enslaved themselves. They may, at times, want to do the right thing, even the Biblical thing, but seem powerless to effect this in their lives. Their minds, emotions and wills have been warped so that they think disjointedly, they emote inanely and they decide timorously. Their crooked nature cries to be straightened out. They need Christ's salvation. They need conversion—a "turning around."

A Gospel That Changes Persons

As the minds, emotions and wills of humans have been warped by sin, so have their *consciences*. A shocking experiment with frogs in the laboratory is illustrative. If you place a frog in a pan of hot water he will leap out immediately. However, if you put the frog in a pan of lukewarm water and slowly heat it, you can boil the frog to death, but it will not leap out of the pan. It becomes so acclimated to the deadly conditions that it is unaware that it is dying. So it is with conscience. A person may become hardened. A conscience can become seared and acclimated to insensitivity. The first time a person cheated, or was immoral, or took something that did not belong to him his conscience was active. Later, if he persisted, the conscience gradually lost sensitivity or "died." Paul speaks the awesome words in Romans that "God gave them up to their sins." This is the anesthetic effect of sinfulness when a person begins to think sin is acceptable or not as bad as it once seemed. The person has lost the ability to tell right from wrong. Everything has become relative, situational. So far-spread is this disease, so totally has it smitten the mentality, emotions, will and conscience of mankind that it can be said that man is "totally depraved."

Total depravity does not imply God's inability to work His miracle in lives. It does not mean life is devoid of hope, but it does point to man's inability to be acceptable before God outside of Jesus Christ.

It also needs to be said that there is a Biblical

difference between "sin" and "sins." Many Christians go through life confusing the two and thus never have a meaningful understanding of God's view. "Sin" is the dispositional word. We are "sinners" by birth and by choice. We need God's help. "Sins," however, are the concomitant or the children of the parent word, sin. Baptists often ask their parishioners in pastor's classes, "Which is cause and which is effect? Does one commit sins and thereby become a sinner, or is one a sinner and therefore commits sins?" The correct answer is basic to an understanding of salvation.

The Biblical answer was given by King David, when he said, "But I was born a sinner, yes, from the moment my mother conceived me" (Ps. 51:5, *The Living Bible*). Prior to sins being committed there is always the dispositional "sin problem" with which we have been born, our sinfulness, which assures wrong choices and leads to the "sins" problem. It might seem a shocking statement, but Jesus did not primarily come to die for "sins" but for "sinners." In other words, His death was to atone for sin—our nature, not our deeds. Indeed, the apostle Paul said, "For God caused Christ, who himself knew nothing of sin, actually to *be* sin for our sakes, so that in Christ we might be made good with the goodness of God" (II Cor. 5:21, Phillips). There you have the basic truth of Scripture!

How often are the "big" sins catalogued—murder, adultery, theft, cheating, and the like—and

A Gospel That Changes Persons

considered the main concerns of God? These are actually the "love-children" of SIN. No one goes to hell primarily because he has murdered, let us say, but because he was a sinner—a murderer in heart—prior to committing the act. The act was perhaps the inevitable effect. A religion that does not change the sinner but only plucks decorously at his sins will not suffice.

Christianity deals with sinners. When Christ saves and converts the sinners of their sin nature, He has automatically covered the "sins" problem. When, through faith in Christ sin is forgiven and the guilt removed, the propensity to commit the individual sins is gone. Christ always gets to the cause while many Christians become obsessed with the effects.

Because of sin, we have been afflicted with physical death. "It is appointed unto men once to die" (Heb. 9:27). Beyond that we are faced with spiritual death. Made for fellowship with God, sin has cut us off from God. We have not broken God's law so much as broken ourselves upon God's law. We are faced with eternal death because of sin.

Jesus spoke more about hell than anyone else in the Bible. He spoke of the hell that was to come. He never inferred that "all the hell we will ever experience is what we are now experiencing on earth." That is wishful thinking. Whatever He meant by hell, we know it is essentially eternal separation from God. "And these shall go away into everlasting punishment" (Mt. 25:46). "The Son of man shall send forth his angels, and they shall gather out of his kingdom all things that offend, and them which do iniquity; And shall cast them into a furnace of fire: there shall be wailing and gnashing of teeth'' (Mt. 13: 41, 42).

So salvation addresses itself to a man's *mind, emotions, will and conscience*. That which is crooked and wrong and deserving of hell becomes right and straightened and assured of Heaven. Christianity, then, is not "ten things you cannot do," or must do—a kind of pilot's checklist before takeoff. Christianity is a person's coming to Jesus Christ in genuine awareness and sorrow for rebellion against God, and a genuine acknowledgment and expectant hope of what God will now do for us as we repent and seek reconciliation. That which has been separated God now brings together again.

First, then, there must be repentance and a turning from our sin to God because "all have sinned, and come short of the glory of God" (Rom. 3: 23) and "the wages of sin is death; but the gift of God is eternal life" (Rom. 6: 23). Since no one can escape being a sinner, and since all sinners have the divine sentence of eternal death on them, everyone needs salvation. A person is a sinner not only by virtue of being part of the sinful human race, but by virtue of his own choice as well (cf. Rom. 3: 9, 10). A person cannot save himself. In Ephesians 2: 1 everyone outside of Jesus Christ is described as being "dead in trespasses and sin." A physically dead person can do

A Gospel That Changes Persons

nothing to help himself; neither can a spiritually dead person.

As a six-year-old boy, I visited, with my family, the famed resort known as Arrowhead Lake in southern California. On one occasion, though I could not swim, I had enjoyed moving hand-over-hand around the boats moored in deep water and working myself out to the boat farthest from the shore. I had been seen by my mother and severely rebuked for this dangerous escapade. On another occasion I decided, with my six-year-old mentality, that my mother did not understand and that I would play with the boats, her warning notwithstanding. I disobeyed her and made my way, hand-over-hand, to the distant boat. At last, as she had warned, my hand slipped and I sank without a cry or a murmur. I felt myself going down into the deep ooze of the lake-bottom. I was horrified with fear and I began swallowing water.

Meanwhile, back on the shore, my mother, who was sunning herself, heard a cry, "There is a little boy in trouble out there." Intuitively she knew it was me, and she ran to the dock where I had been.

Now notice what happened. She did not stand there and say to me as I surfaced, gasping, "Now, son, you are a naughty boy for disobeying me and if you will just quit this foolishness and get to shore I will give you a good spanking." Nor did she stand there, hands on her hips, waiting for me to rise to the surface so that she could begin a lecture on "How to

THE BAPTIST HERITAGE

Swim." Nor did she jump in beside me and, taking long strokes toward shore, yell, "Dear, just do what I am doing and you will make it into shore safely." She did none of these perhaps well-meaning things. She knew that I was drowning. I would die. I could not save myself. The more I tried to save myself, the worse my situation became. So she immediately dove into the waters, down, down to the bottom of the lake where she found me. Getting a fistful of my hair, she pulled me to the surface and took me to shore, pumped the water out of me, and loved me like I hadn't been loved before. In that act she pictured what Christians down through the ages call the "redeeming grace of God." She had done for me what I could not do for myself.

Jesus Christ came to my rescue . . . wading out into the middle of my muddle . . . coming to me at my address in a way I could understand . . . dying my death for me so that if I truly believed in Him and received Him into my life I might become a new creature, a changed person, like Him, who becomes involved in changing my world around me (II Cor. 5:17). As we repent or show godly sorrow for our sins, and confess them to God, and believe that He will cleanse and forgive, we have His assurance that those who come will not be turned away (Jn. 6:37).

That is good news. My acceptance of God's gift, Jesus Christ, and His acceptance of me is what it means to be "born again." A new life has begun. A new person has emerged in the likeness of Jesus

A Gospel That Changes Persons

Himself. What ineffable, inexpressible joy it is to know the "peace *of* God" (Phil. 4:7) because we have made "peace *with* God" (Rom. 5:1).

This is common Christian doctrine. However, not all Christians have stressed what Baptists refer to as "the priesthood of the believer." From Smyth, Helwys, Williams and Clark to the present day, soul-competency, that is, the ability of the individual to come to God without the help of priests, ministers, or other ecclesiastical persons or procedures, has been emphasized. This is not to say that clergymen or other Christians might not be instrumental and, indeed, of great value in helping a person come to God. It is, however, axiomatic to Baptists that no one need have a human intermediary between God and man. "There is only one God, and only one intermediary between God and men, the Man Christ Jesus" (I Tim. 2:5, Phillips). At any moment or in any place anyone can cry out to God from his heart, and God will hear the prayer of sincere penitence.

This concept of "the priesthood of the believer" has long been one of the Baptist distinctives. It stemmed not only from Scripture, but from the strong Baptist emphasis upon personal responsibility and soul-freedom.

In conclusion, we should remind ourselves that conversion can take on fraudulent forms. There are at least three phony views of conversion about which Baptists have tried to be vigilantly aware. A "theological conversion" is trading off one cluster of ideas for another cluster. For example, a skeptic claims he cannot have faith in God, in Christ, the Bible or immortality because of his doubt of their validity. Later he becomes converted to new ideas, new rational explanations that seem to make sense, and he supposedly embraces Christianity. He has merely swapped ideas. He has had a theological conversion by way of his reason and ideas, but nothing has necessarily happened to change his lifestyle, his behavior, his feelings, or his personhood.

This is not to say that theological ideas are unimportant, but that they should never be ends in themselves. Rather, theology must always be a means to an end. It shows us where we need to go. It points to the Lamb of God, who alone can take away the sin of the world.

"Conversion-to-a-feeling" is the second phony view against which we need be on guard. A touching story, or a Biblical truth powerfully told might elicit tremendous surges of emotional response within a person, but there must be more than sentiment in Biblical conversion. Tears, laughter, sorrow may go along with true conversion, in individual cases, but they should not be the end in themselves. Some people, in reciting their conversion experience, stress euphoric feelings. Feelings are not wrong. Indeed, they are precious to remember, but a conversion *based* on feeling—a thrill, a glow, or tears—is not valid. Many reasons can exist in a situation which effect a conversion-to-feeling: mob psy-

A Gospel That Changes Persons

chology, touching music, tender stories, deep-seated inner personal needs of a person at just the right time. In moments of such intense emotion one is readily set up for a conversion-to-feeling. But it must be said that this also is a phony conversion if there is no real, lasting behavior change into the likeness of Jesus Christ.

The third fraudulent conversion might be called "a moral conversion." When a person has lived an immoral life and, for whatever reason, changes to a moral life-style, he has had a moral conversion. A change of moral ideals has taken place, but that is all. He has not had a Christian conversion. Now, all of this is not to say that either theology, feelings or morals are insignificant. But it is to say that no combination of the three, or any of them taken singly, can provide a Christian conversion. Not one of these phony conversions can take one outside himself. We are left as subjectively alone as ever with our feelings, our ideas, our morals. A person needs Jesus Christ to give meaning and direction to his life. Only in Jesus Christ has God revealed His divine plan for human life. We cannot be satisfied with knowing *about* Jesus Christ. We must know Him in personal commitment as our Lord, Savior and personal friend who will never leave us nor forsake us. He must be the center of our existence. He is the one who can remove our sins from us "as far as the East is from the West." He is our God who promises, "I will not remember your sins." He buries our sins into the sea of His forgetfulness. He makes us whole.

Baptists have died for this life-changing Gospel that sets men free—free to be like Jesus Christ as they relate to God and to their fellowmen. It was Walter Rauschenbusch, famed Baptist of the mid-1800s, who stated so succinctly:

> The Christian faith as Baptists hold it sets spiritual experience boldly to the front as the one great thing in Christianity. It aims at experimental faith. We are an evangelistic body. We summon all men to conscious repentance from sin, to prayer for forgiveness. We ask a man: "Have you put your faith in Christ? Have you submitted your will to His will? Have you received the inward assurance that your sins are forgiven and that you are at peace with God? Have you had experience of God?" (Taken from his "Why I Am a Baptist," 1898.)

Yes, Baptists believe in a Gospel that changes persons, and through persons changes the home, the power structures of society, and finally the whole world. But, it must be stressed, God is the initiator and change begins in the heart and life of the individual person as he offers his affirmative "yes" to God's invitation "to come unto me."

Questions for Thought and Discussion

1. How do you define "repentance" and "faith"? Are they two separate "events" or are they aspects of the same thing?

A Gospel That Changes Persons

2. Why did God create a world where it was possible for man to sin? Can you support your answer with teachings from the Bible?

3. What is the ultimate cause of sin in human lives? Why?

4. If church attendance, good deeds, and belief in the existence of God don't make a person a Christian, what does?

5. How would you answer this question: "Does one commit sins and thereby become a sinner, or is one a sinner and therefore commits sins?"

6. Describe in your own words what Jesus does to change the individual from being a sinner to a "born again" son of God.

7. What do Baptists mean by "the priesthood of the believer"?

Suggestions for Further Study

Norman H. Maring, *American Baptists Whence and Whither* (Valley Forge: Judson Press, 1968), pp. 81-84.

8

Members of a Body

IT IS IMPERATIVE TO UNDERSTAND the nature and work of the Church if we are to properly comprehend the purpose of God, His method of grace, and the work of the Holy Spirit. Baptists have affirmed that the Church of Jesus Christ is one body of believers consisting of those persons past, present and future who affirm, experientially, that Jesus Christ is their Lord and Savior. But the Body—Christ's Church—inevitably takes variant forms that have led to the development of denominations. Baptists, however, have not been threatened by different points of view. Indeed, they have been in the vanguard of the discussion of varied views, believing that in the forum of ideas, when guided by the Holy Scriptures, we come to a better understanding of God's truth. This fact should not mislead one into believing that Baptists have been placid eclectics, doctrinally, putting "a

Members of a Body

little of this 'n that" together as the basis of faith. Far from it. However, while recognizing minor or even major differences with people of other groups who have had a deep faith in the Savior, they have allowed the common depth of commitment to Jesus Christ to override many minor differences. The essential oneness in Christ as Savior and Lord has been the basis of the Baptists' view of the Church Universal.

What is the Church? The word which is regularly translated "Church" in the New Testament is *ekklesia,* a Greek word with a basic meaning of "the called out." It came to refer to an assembly or meeting of persons. The early Christian church and the first Baptists of England applied it to themselves. They believed that they had been called out of the world and given God's message of redeeming love and grace as revealed in the life, death and resurrection of Jesus Christ. They were called to proclaim and to demonstrate the Word of the Lord. It is particularly important to note that the word "church" never refers to a building. Rather, it refers to a people, a "called people." In other words, church is not *a place* you visit on Sundays for worship; it is the *group of people* of which you become a member through your life in Jesus Christ. If you have a valid experience with Jesus Christ, through faith *you* are a part of the Church.

The Church is seen, then, essentially as those for whom Christ came and died (Eph. 5:25). Indeed,

God purchased His Church at the cost of Christ's blood (Acts 20:28). As the Christian enters into the life of the Church he finds the various ministries of grace, the means of growth, and his own area of service.

Basic to any study of the Church must be the concept of a "covenant people." A covenant is a promise that binds both parties involved into a relationship governed by certain responsibilities; it further stipulates that the parties will perform the responsibilities toward each other that their relationship demands. God provided a covenant to Abraham in Genesis 17, a chapter of great importance for an understanding of the Church since this covenant is the basis of the Church's life in both Testaments.

When Christ came to our earthly scene the Old Testament promise was fulfilled. Yet, the New Testament church is, historically, a continuation of the Old Testament Israel. But now Christ assumed the role of Mediator of the covenant and was Himself the connection between the Mosaic and Christian phases of this covenant. The New Testament shows Him to be the true Israel of God, the seed of Abraham in whom all nations of the earth receive blessing (Gal. 3:8; 14-29). Christ's death did away with the Old Testament sacrificial system forever. Those who believe in Him, be they Jews or Gentiles, become the people of God on earth. Baptism became the initiatory sign, a correlary to circumcision in the Old Testament. It typifies the union of the believer with

Members of a Body

Christ in His death, burial and resurrection, which union is the means of entry into the Church (Rom. 6:3ff; Gal. 3:27; Col. 2:11-13).

As the old Israel was called to be God's "own possession," "a kingdom of priests," "a holy nation," so also is the new Israel, the Church of Jesus Christ, of which every believer is a part (Ex. 19:5, 6; I Peter 2:9). We have become "Abraham's seed," "the Israel of God" (Gal. 3:29; 6:16; cf. Rom. 4:11-18). This New Israel is in no sense an ethnic or geographical entity. Its origin is from above; it is a nation whose citizenship is in Heaven.

Paul the apostle thoroughly concurred with Peter's "people of God" emphasis, but in his preaching and teaching he preferred the concept of the "body of Christ." He focused upon the organic character of the Church, with its members belonging to one another even as organs of a body belong to each other (cf. Eph. 1:22, 23; 4:4, 11, 12, 15, 16). That Body, the Church, is viewed as the medium of communication with the world as well as an organic unity so indissolubly linked that any division harms the entire Body. Christ is the Head of the Body (Col. 1:18), and to belong to Christ is to belong to His body, His Church. From the New Testament standpoint, a Christian living in isolation is unthinkable, if not a contradiction in terms. Thus Baptists continually refer to being part of the New Testament Church in that we are enunciating our ties with the Day of Pentecost when the Holy Spirit came upon all

THE BAPTIST HERITAGE

those who were in prayer in the Upper Room following Christ's ascension (Acts 2).

This Body that Paul sees as the Church consists of a diversity in unity. That is Paul's predominant thought in Romans 12 and I Corinthians 12—14 which declare that God has given different gifts and diverse functions to the members of the Body, the Church. No one member holds supremacy over another by virtue of exercising his gift just as no one part of the human body lords it over another. Organic unity is as basic to the health of the Church as it is to the body's health.

From these teachings, Baptists have clearly seen their obligation. There are diversities of ministries or services. Those in leadership lead in humility and love as servants (Rom. 12: 3-8; I Cor. 12: 4-31; Lk. 22: 26). But all Christians are to be responsible participants in the holy priesthood of our Lord and Savior. All Christians offer "spiritual sacrifices"—a dedicated life to God. All Christians proclaim God's "wonderful deeds" and become the ambassadors of Christ in the world (cf. I Pet. 2: 10; II Cor. 5: 14-20).

We have seen how Paul refers to the Church as Christ's *building*, now growing into "an holy temple in the Lord" (Eph. 2: 21), and His *body*, now growing into full maturity (Rom. 12; I Cor. 12; Eph. 4: 11, 12). Paul also describes the Church as Christ's *bride*, now being prepared and cleansed in preparation for "the marriage supper of the Lamb" (Eph.

Members of a Body

5:25ff). The New Testament uses other names for the Church such as "the house of God," "the habitation of God," "God's husbandry," "the Church of God," "the Israel of God," "the flock of God," "the New Jerusalem," "the family in Heaven," "a mystery," "the light of the world," "the salt of the earth," and others. A study of the Biblical names for the Church makes for a fascinating eye-opener to its real nature.

One of our difficulties in thinking about the Church is that our first confrontation with it is usually organizational. As we have seen, organization does not make the Church what it is. The local church is part of a larger body which may manifest itself locally through organizational structures, but the emphasis is placed upon the organism. Indeed, the organizational form in some churches might actually disguise the true nature of the church rather than manifesting it. Essentially, the Church has not found its origin in human organization but in the divine creativity of God who has called common sinners into a precious fellowship with their Savior and Lord. So, with the apostle Paul, we might say that the real life of the Church, like its individual members, is for now "hid with Christ in God" (Col. 3:3). At the end of history, when Christ appears again in glory, the full nature of the Church will be revealed in power and glory.

It needs to be repeated, then, that the early Baptists held a lofty view of the Church. It was God's

THE BAPTIST HERITAGE

creation consisting of believers only. It was not a "Baptist" church (or any other label) but the Church of Jesus Christ in which all believers have their place.

John Smyth, early forebear of the Baptists, published a confession of faith in 1610 under the title "Propositions and Conclusions Concerning True Christian Religion Conteyning a Confession of Faith of Certaine English People, Livinge at Amsterdam." His life was drawing to a close when he formulated this series of Articles concerning the Church. Article 69 comprises perhaps the most famous words Smyth ever wrote when he said:

> I believe that all penitent and faithfull Christians are brethren in the communion of the outward church, whersoever they live, by what name soever they are knowen, which in truth and zeale, follow repentance and faith, though compassed with never so manie ignorances and infirmaties: and we salute them all with a holie kisse, being hartilie grieved that wee which follow after one faith, and one spirit, one Lord, and one God, one bodie, and one baptisme, should be rent into so manie sects, and schismes: and that only for matters of lesse moment.

These words capture the true sentiment of most Baptists down through the centuries with respect to the Church of our Lord.

John Robinson also wrote a book in 1610, enti-

Members of a Body

tled, *Justification of Separation from the Church of England* in which Robinson punctuated a very controversial point held by some Baptists and deplored by others, when he commented:

> There is no true visible church of Christ, but a particular congregation only... Every true visible church of Christ or ordinary assembly of the faithful, hath, by Christ's ordinance, power in itself immediately under Christ to elect, to ordain, deprive and depose their ministers, and to execute all other ecclesiastical censures.

It was Robinson's spirit and concept that raised an important question, "Where does the local church (with a small *c*) enter the picture? It is well and good to believe in the Church Universal—the body of believers in Jesus Christ—but what about the local church with its buildings and its organizational structures? Are these not part of the Church of Jesus Christ?"

Baptists, perhaps more than most denominations, have insisted that the local church be autonomous and self-directing, and yet affirm its relationship to the larger organism—the Church Universal. They have declared their freedom from ecclesiastical hierarchies and the encumbrance of any body of administration "higher" than the local congregation. Thus, in one of the first Baptist Confessions drawn up by seven London congregations in 1644, we hear the words:

THE BAPTIST HERITAGE

> And although the particular Congregations be distinct and severall Bodies, every one a compact and knit Citie in itselfe; yet are they all to walk by one and the same Rule, and by all means convenient to have the counsell and help one of another in all needfull affaires of the Church, as members of one body in the common faith under Christ their onely head (XLVII).

So one cannot speak of "The Baptist Church" in the same sense that one might speak of "The Catholic Church" or "The Lutheran Church." The Baptist denominations exist by consent of their local churches. If the local churches so desired they could vote their denomination into nonexistence. The local church sits in autonomous control over its own program and ministry as under the Lord and the Scriptures. It may choose to affiliate itself with a denomination, or it may decide to be independent of denominational organizations. But the choice is the congregation's, and it is not in the organizational hands of an ecclesiastical authority.

Thus Baptists have made a distinction between the terms "churches" and "Church." Does a believer belong to the organism (Church) or the organization (church)? In most instances he will be found in both. However, there are some Christians who never find it in their hearts to unite with a local church, but nonetheless are part of the organism of Christ's Body (though this tends to make them irresponsible and isolated, rather than loving, relational children of

Members of a Body

God). Conversely, there are many who join the organization (local church) who are not citizens of the Kingdom of Heaven; they are trusting in organization without being part of the organism. Perhaps this is what Paul had in mind when he enjoined the church in II Corinthians 13:5, "Examine yourselves, whether ye be in the faith."

Baptists have affirmed from the beginning that participation in Christ's Church depended upon the recognition and acceptance of three essentials: repentance of sin, faith in Jesus Christ, confession by baptism (Acts 2: 38-41; 3: 19; 4: 12). To love is to do, to be, to participate in the life of the Body in its manifestation as a local group of believers who have banded together for worship, fellowship, study and service. A Christian is an activist in the best sense of the term. He relates, he serves, he cares. He utilizes his God-given gifts for the advancement of the Body of Christ—His Church.

There will always be critics of the church. In Boccaccio's *Decameron* there is the story of a Christian who was seeking to win a Jewish friend to Christ. The Jew seemed unusually obstinate. Just as the Christian was about to give up in his attempt, the Jew mentioned that he was going to Rome to view the church at its very center, prior to making any decision. Knowing of the corruption, immorality and greed of Rome in those days, the Christian was abashed at this announcement and could not think of a worse place for his Jewish friend to go to determine the matter of genuine Christianity. However, he was both shocked and surprised when his Jewish friend returned some time later with the announcement that he was going to join the church as a direct result of having visited Rome. When asked what it was that brought him to such an important decision the Jew said, "If the church has survived so many years with all that terrible corruption at its heart, then it surely must be divine!"

As difficult as it may be to understand and as imperfect as today's church seems to be, God is yet using it in His plan for the redemption of the world. William Keucher's work, *An Exodus for the Church*, shares an Associated Press dispatch, from Pittsburg, Kansas, which reported the following amusing incident:

> Mount Carmel Hospital here has a small building which contains a gasoline-driven generator which can be started up quickly should electrical power fail for a time at the four-story medical facility.
>
> Recently, power failed and all electrical units in the hospital halted, including the elevators. In one of the elevators, which was stopped between floors, a trapped man began pounding on the doors of the cage and shouting for help. A nurse, thinking to calm down the caged man, said, "Don't be alarmed, the maintenance man will soon get the auxiliary unit started and we will have power again." But inside the cage came a shout: "I am the maintenance man!!"

Members of a Body

The point is illustrative of the situation in which many church leaders find themselves today. They are being counted upon for the restoration of the power, the purity and Spirit-filled leadership needed for these perilous times. Yet, it would appear that more often than not they are the very ones bogged down, trapped within the mechanical failures of their organizational structures. As long as a sinful humanity is in existence the church will manifest the weakness of those constituting it. In spite of that, however, God is guarding His truth, calling out His remnant, bringing together His people in marvelous and exciting ways.

Questions for Thought and Discussion

1. How do Baptists define "the Church"? What are its essential characteristics?
2. What does the covenant that God made with Abraham (Genesis 17) have to do with the Church today?
3. Why does the author say that "from the New Testament standpoint, a Christian living in isolation is unthinkable, if not a contradiction in terms"?
4. What is the relationship between the local church or congregation of believers and the universal Church?
5. Why is it incorrect to speak of "the Baptist Church" in the same way that one might speak of "the Catholic Church"?

Suggestions for Further Study

Edwin S. Gaustad, "The Backus-Leland Tradition," *Baptist Concepts of the Church*, op. cit., pp. 106-134.

9

Popes, Pastors, and Presbyters

IT IS IN THE CONTEXT of the local church that the gifts of the Holy Spirit for ministry are usually discovered and practiced by the individual (cf. I Cor. 12 and Eph. 4). The local church is the training center where the believer becomes better equipped for his specific ministry to the world. For it is in the world that he must be the church, live out his Gospel, and point men to Christ. The church is not a religious retirement center or a comfortable place to which one escapes from the traumas of the world. It is a place of fellowship, worship and service, where we are renewed, invigorated, inspired and energized to go out and *be* Christ's Church throughout the week. The progression in the New Testament is always *toward* the world and not *away* from it. The world is precisely the arena where our faith is to be daily demonstrated. We dare not become consumers of

God's love. We must be active conduits of His love—in a sense, producers of it, as we allow Him to flow through us.

Local churches are appointed by God to be the local manifestations of the invisible Church or the Body of Christ on earth. Yet it is hard to determine what the actual structure or form of this local church should be. Historically, there are few details that seem to reveal a consistent pattern of church life during the apostolic era. One can find Biblical language that seems to be suggestive of a more central, episcopal or presbyterian form of government, while at the same time, there are many allusions to democracy at work in congregational forms of government. Baptists have adhered to the latter forms throughout their history.

The espousal of this life-style has implications for other areas of church life as well. Baptists have historically shunned the use of creeds. This is not to say that they have shown insensitivity to the value of such doctrinal statements. Indeed, they have used them to express the Church's faith in a given situation or point in time. But they don't consider a creed binding upon the conscience of believers as the New Testament is. A Baptist is free to agree or disagree with any creed.

The prime factor within the life of the first-century churches was not a dependence upon organizational structures, because there were very few forms to follow. There was, however, a burning awareness

Popes, Pastors, and Presbyters

that Christ was present and alive, moving in their midst. Their enthusiasm, and the indomitable spirit that kept them going against all odds for the centuries that followed, flowed from this awareness of the personal Christ living within His Church. Many of those first-century Christians had seen the Lord. Besides the apostles, hundreds had observed the resurrected Christ as He taught them, following that first Easter morning.

These early churches, then, were fraternities of deep faith that had banded together in study, worship, fellowship and ministry. There were virtually no offices that demanded special privileges or deference. There were only the eager voluntary services rendered in such a way that it became increasingly obvious that some of the church members were unusually gifted by God. This inevitably elevated such persons to leadership, with the rest assuming a committed fellowship of participants.

The formal emergence of leaders with official positions and titles came at a later date, after some of the original glow and freshness of the Resurrection had waned. It is not difficult to understand, from our vantage point, how any emphasis upon qualitative differences between leaders and their followers would become dangerous. Such prominence would certainly lead to excesses in which these leaders would be viewed, by some, as having the right to dispense grace and forgiveness. This was never the intention of God, nor the teaching of Scripture, nor

THE BAPTIST HERITAGE

the deliberate intent of the early church; yet history reveals that it happened. The danger was not understood by the first-century church. Their delightful emphasis upon the Gospel and its proclamation overshadowed such mundane things as "dangers" that might accrue from the forms of leadership.

Yet even as leaders emerged there was an amazing sense of equality in the local churches. They remembered their Lord's statement:

> In this world the kings and great men order their slaves around, and the slaves have no choice but to like it! But among you, the one who serves you best will be your leader (Lk. 22:25, 26, TLB).
>
> How they enjoy the deference paid them on the streets, and to be called 'Rabbi' and 'Master'! Don't ever let anyone call you that. For only God is your Rabbi and all of you are on the same level, as brothers. And don't address anyone here on earth as 'Father,' for only God in heaven should be addressed like that. And don't be called 'Master,' for only one is your master, even the Messiah. The more lowly your service to others, the greater you are. To be the greatest, be a servant. But those who think themselves great shall be disappointed and humbled; and those who humble themselves shall be exalted (Mt. 23:7-12, TLB).

Eventually, two offices arose out of necessity: "pastor" and "deacon." Interestingly, a careful study of Acts 6 reveals these offices did not provide power or dominance for ruling the church. Rather they were established for service.

Pastors needed to tend certain significant aspects of ministry such as study, preparing messages, praying, developing a closeness with God, and delivering God's instructions to the people. So that their pastors might be freed to do these things, deacons were called out of the ranks according to explicit standards conveyed in I Timothy 3:8-13. Deacon meant "servant" or "helper." The deacons were to serve by visitation, tending and counseling widows and orphans, the destitute and the infirm. They were to be valued assistants to the pastors in ministering.

The New Testament used the words "bishop," "elder," and "pastor" for the person who guided the church. The term "pastor" conveys a shepherd-sheep relationship, which Baptists have zealously espoused through the years. The pastor was to provide spiritual food for the flock and oversee their needs and life-styles. He was to be, as nearly as possible, an embodiment of Jesus Christ. The words "bishop" and "elder" denote other aspects of the pastoral ministry, as when the pastor had to function as an administrative guide. "Elder" conveys maturity, widsom and commitment—the kinds of qualities necessary in a church leader. "Bishop" or "overseer" indicates the nature of the work to be accomplished. Indeed, in the New Testament there seemed to be bishops in almost every local church (Acts 14:23; 20:17; Phil. 1:1; Titus 1:5; Jas. 5:14).

THE BAPTIST HERITAGE

In Titus 1:5-8 the words "elder" and "bishop" are interchangeable. Acts 20:17-28 reminds us that these leaders are to tend the membership's spiritual development. Thus, we conclude that elders, bishops and pastors have the same responsibility.

As the world grew in complexity it demanded a multiphased ministry far beyond anything the first-century church could imagine. Boards of trustees, missions, music and Christian education, to name but a few, were developed to give additional leadership and emphasis to the many aspects of ministry arising from the needs of people. Persons serving on such boards or committees have been functioning servants or deacons whether given that technical name or not. They were assistants to the pastors in a very significant manner for the overall ministry of the church.

The ordination of pastors gradually arose out of the need to raise and preserve the quality of ministry. Standards were needed. In Baptist churches, ordination by a hierarchy of church potentates has never existed. Ministers are ordained or "set apart" to the Gospel ministry by the approval of the local congregation as the individual candidate for ministry shows evidence that he is genuinely called of God.

The normal procedure in most Baptist churches provides for the candidate to be interviewed by the pastor and/or the board of deacons who make a recommendation to the local congregation; the congregation may approve or disapprove. If the candidate is approved, he is presented to a screening committee of other Baptist brethren from either the region or association. He is questioned by them about his personal faith, his call to ministry, and his academic and spiritual qualifications for ministry. If the screening committee of the association or region approves the candidate, a recommendation is referred back to the local church which calls an Ordination Council and issues an invitation to all the Baptist churches in the area or association to send delegates on a specific date for the express purpose of examining the candidate. When the council is convened, the delegates question the candidate along the same general lines as the screening committee has done, focusing on his conversion, his call, and his doctrinal and academic background. If the candidate is approved by the council, they recommend that the local church start ordination procedures. The local church usually invites her sister congregations in the area to share in the joyous occasion of setting apart their candidate to ministry.

During the ordination service, following appropriate comments adjuring the candidate to be faithful in his ministry, and the local congregation to be faithful in their support of his leadership, a certificate of ordination is granted to the new minister. A record of the ordination is kept in denominational files.

The entire process rests in the hands of the local church. They began the proceedings and they conclude them. They invited their sister churches of like faith to join them in the interrogation and celebration, but they, nonetheless, held the right to ordain or not to ordain. This has been and is Baptist polity. The people have been led by God to speak their mind and exercise their collective authority through democratic processes.

Normally, ordination is for life. A minister, however, may, and often does, surrender his credentials of ordination, should circumstances cause him to leave his ministry.

As Baptists continued their study of God's Word they found two ordinances inaugurated by their Lord—Baptism and the Lord's Supper—which have become an integral part of their church life. Let us deal with baptism first.

Baptism is no spurious accretion as have been some other customs of the Church. It is the great initiatory rite of early Christendom brought down through the centuries, wherein a believer professes his faith by the baptismal act, identifying himself with Christ. It is included in the Great Commission (Mt. 28:19, 20; Mk. 16:15, 16) and the apostles took Christ's words seriously, as is evidenced on the Day of Pentecost. Under the conviction of Peter's magnificent sermon, the multitudes cried out, "What shall we do?" Peter replied, "Repent, and be baptized" (Acts 2:38).

From the very beginning, Baptists have held that baptism was for believers only. In virtually all instances regarding baptism the Scripture shows that those baptized had first experienced and acknowledged the Lord Jesus Christ as personal Savior. The order found in the New Testament is always: repentance, faith, then baptism. Baptism, for one who has not received Christ into his life, would be an unholy mockery of God's truth.

Baptism, then, is an ordinance to be practiced within the church to show Christ's death, burial and resurrection. The person who has received Christ is, symbolically, "buried" (Rom. 6: 4) with Christ and raised with Him. He is saying, "I want my old life to be dead and buried with Christ. I long to be raised up by the same resurrection power of Jesus Christ to live my life in His strength and in His life-style." Baptists believe that Scripture clearly teaches that baptism, in and of itself, has no saving power. If an unbeliever goes through the waters of baptism, all that has happened is that a dry sinner becomes a wet sinner. No inner change has taken place. The external act of water baptism has no transformational powers.

What about the mode of baptism? The word "baptize," both in the New Testament and in Greek literature, according to 40 major lexicons, means "dip" or "immerse." However, the mode of baptism is not predicated upon lexicons, or even the Scriptural injunction alone. There is also historical data that confirms immersion as the mode used by virtually all churches up into the middle ages. Pouring, or affusion, according to the "Teaching of the Twelve Apostles," a second-century document, was permissible if water were scarce. Sprinkling was an even later development.

Herbert Lockyer, in *All the Doctrines of the Bible*, says:

> Well, let's look at what scholarly men who upheld the view of infant baptism have to say regarding the exact New Testament mode of baptism, and by doing so we shall find that such scholars range themselves on the side of immersion without partiality or force.
>
> *Martin Luther*. The words of this reformer are remarkable—"I would wish that such as are to be baptized should be completely immersed into water, according to the meaning of the word and the significance of the ordinance."
>
> *Dean Stanley*. This famous scholar and writer said—"There can be no question that the original form of baptism—the very meaning of the word—was complete immersion in the deep baptismal waters."
>
> *Sanday and Headlam*. In their powerful work on Romans, these two gifted expositors express this interpretation of Romans 6:4—"It (baptism) expresses symbolically a series of acts corresponding to the redeeming acts of Christ. Immersion—death. Submersion—burial (ratification of death). Emergence—resurrection."

Dr. Marcus Dods. This notable Presbyterian, adding to a quotation of Bishop Lightfoot's, where he also argues for immersion—"To use the Pauline language, his old man is dead and buried in the water and he rises from this cleansing grave a new man. The full significance of the rite would have been lost had immersion not been practiced."

Professor Lindsay. As another outstanding scholar and non-immersionist, he adds a striking quote to the New Testament mode of immersion—"It may be admitted at once that immersion, where the whole body including the head is plunged into a pool of pure water, gives a more vivid picture of the cleansing of the soul from sin: and that complete surrounding with water suits better the metaphors of burial in Romans 6:4 and Colossians 2:12, and being surrounded by the cloud in I Corinthians 10:2."

These statements—and passages of Scripture such as Matthew 3:6; Mark 1:5; and Acts 8:38—appear, to those of the Baptist position, to dictate immersion as the normative Biblical mode.

With respect to infant baptism, Baptists can only say that the Bible does not make a direct pronouncement. In the case of the Philippian jailor's household (Acts 16:33, 34), there is no implication that infants were included, nor do any other passages make direct statements with regard to infant baptism.

Baptism, then, as practiced by the Baptists throughout their history, has been that moment in a

THE BAPTIST HERITAGE

Christian's life when he makes a public, irrevocable commitment to Jesus Christ, through whose death he has been saved, and by whose life he will be enabled to daily live the Christian life. He has taken a stride in the faith that need not be repeated. It is a one-time event. He has made a formal announcement, in action, of his new relationship with Jesus Christ, and has also declared his entrance into the redeemed community which constitutes the Church of our Lord.

Baptism should be indicative of God's calling us, not to a place or position, but to a journey; not to a triumph, but to new, exciting toils; not to a permanent status, but to an ever-expanding becoming; not to a niche in life, but to God Himself. To revert back to the old sins of the past life is unthinkable. They are to be abandoned by God's strength. Holiness or conscious spiritual growth is engendered by study of the Word of God, fellowship with the saints, worship in the house of God, and service to mankind within the arena of everyday life. In Colossians 2: 12, 13, 20—3: 2 (*The Living Bible*) the great apostle proclaims:

> For in baptism you see how your old, evil nature died with him and was buried with him; and then you came up out of death with him into a new life because you trusted the Word of the mighty God who raised Christ from the dead. You were dead in sins, and your sinful desires were not yet cut away.

Then he gave you a share in the very life of Christ, for he forgave all your sins . . . Since you died, as it were, with Christ and this has set you free from following the world's ideas of how to be saved—by doing good and obeying various rules—why do you keep right on following them anyway, still bound by such rules as not eating, tasting, or even touching certain foods? Such rules are mere human teachings, for food was made to be eaten and used up. These rules may seem good, for rules of this kind require strong devotion and are humiliating and hard on the body, but they have no effect when it comes to conquering a person's evil thoughts and desires. They only make him proud. Since you became alive again, so to speak, when Christ arose from the dead, now set your sights on the rich treasures and joys of heaven where he sits beside God in the place of honor and power. Let heaven fill your thoughts; don't spend your time worrying about things down here.

As to the Lord's Supper or Communion, we have what Baptists have considered the second ordinance of the church. The Lord's Supper is a memorial service inaugurated by our Lord on the eve of His death. As He celebrated the Passover with His men He offered them bread and wine saying, "This is my body," and, "This is my blood of the new testament, which is shed for many" (Mk. 14:22, 24).

In studying I Corinthians 11:23-26, we find that the Lord's Supper had become central to the first-century worship service. There was no Scriptural injunction as to the frequency for this celebration, but it should surely be often enough to keep before the Christian the centrality of Christ's death for sin, and in a very precious, meaningful way lead the believer to a new dimension of commitment.

There are at least three views of the Lord's Supper. The first is widely accepted within the Catholic tradition and is referred to as *transubstantiation* after the change which takes place in the "substance" of the elements of the Lord's Supper—it is asserted that the elements become the body and blood of the Lord. This is an attempt to explain, in philosophic terms, the meaning of Christ's words, "This is my body," and, "This is my blood." The change is held to take place as the priest pronounces Christ's words. By "substance," this view means to indicate the true reality of the elements as opposed to their subsidiary qualities, that is, their specific, perceptible characteristics (i.e., the taste, feel, and nutritional value of bread). This view, though it may seem to espouse cannibalism or dissolve in doubletalk, is an honest attempt to explain a mystery by using the intellectual tools of its day. Baptists, as most Protestants, have rejected this view, however, because of the theological and practical problems associated with it.

Lutherans and some others have held to what is called *consubstantiation*. This view sees the body and blood of Christ as being truly present "in, with, or under" the elements. The proponents of this view

Popes, Pastors, and Presbyters

are not concerned to speculate how this is so, but simply wish to state what they see as theological truth. The presence is by virtue of Christ's Word rather than the priest's consecration.

Baptists believe that the bread only *symbolizes* Christ's body, as the wine only symbolizes His blood. There is symbolism—nothing more or less. Yet, it is precious, sacred symbolism of the highest order, and it is to be regarded with all carefulness and loving reverence. The prime significance of Communion is to symbolize Christ's death as the seal of the New Covenant between God and man. Christ's body being broken on the cross and the shedding of His blood were the means whereby atonement for sin was effected. Just as the bread and the wine are taken into our bodies as we eat and drink together in the Lord's Supper celebration, and as they contribute to our well-being physically, so the Person of Christ enters, spiritually, into our lives at every moment of faith and trust, and communes with us intimately. By this gracious act of God the Christian is constantly being strengthened and learns dependency upon God's grace and strength for daily life.

While there is no more power to save a man's soul in the Lord's Supper than there is in Baptism, yet there is great blessing and an awareness of God's constant presence with His children as we meditate on His grace toward us and as we evidence maturity in our obedience to His teaching. The symbols help us focus our meditation. To not partake of the Lord's

Supper has nothing to do with being shut off from the means of grace. Indeed, a Christian grown cold or careless in his daily life should abstain from the Lord's Supper on certain occasions if he is out of fellowship with the Lord and his fellow believers. But this abstinence should spur him to confession of sin and a renewal of fellowship. Fellow believers find closeness through the celebration of communion because their hearts are being made right as they meditate on God's goodness. However, the Lord's Supper was not inaugurated to bring believers together so much as to bring us to God. A sense of love and camaraderie results, but this is not the primary purpose.

The Lord's Supper, then, is obviously for believers whose hearts and lives are being made right by the grace of God. It is not an ordinance reserved to a local group of believers. It is for all believers who are trusting in Jesus Christ as Lord and Savior.

In terms of cooperation with other Christians of varying denominations, Baptists have ordinarily taken a deliberately open stance, as can be seen in the teaching of some of the great Baptists.

John Bunyan was a Baptist, without apology. Yet he did not give believer's baptism the high place most Baptists did at that time. He wrote a book entitled, *Differences in Judgment about Water Baptism No Bar to Communion* (1673). Also, he wrote *Peaceable Principles and True* (1674). In this latter work he says:

Popes, Pastors, and Presbyters

> Since you would know by what name I would be distinguished from others, I tell you I would be, and hope I am, a Christian, a believer, or other such name which is approved by the Holy Ghost. And as for those titled Anabaptists, Independents, Presbyterians, or the like, I conclude that they came neither from Jerusalem, nor Antioch, but rather from hell and Babylon, for they naturally tend to divisions. You may know them by their fruits.

To John Bunyan, a man was to be known by his life and personal commitment to Jesus Christ, and that was all that was significant. Thus, Bunyan had no problem in accepting infant baptism as well as believer's baptism. Baptism was not a primary consideration for him. As a matter of fact, Bunyan did not see any particular need for a Baptist denomination.

Not many Baptists, though, would want to side with John Bunyan in this, even though he was perhaps one of the most significant voices for the Baptists in the 17th century. The critical thing to note concerning John Bunyan's demur with respect to baptism is that he was a forerunner of many who have longed to move over and cross denominational lines, to work with fellow Evangelicals, and to break through the divisive walls of minor doctrines.

Robert Hall, another noted Baptist preacher, had a significant impact upon the Baptist cause when in 1815 he wrote a pamphlet entitled "Terms of Communion." Then in 1818 he penned "A Further Vindication of the Practice of Free Communion." He, like Bunyan, felt that Baptists should recognize and respect their fellow believers who were not Baptists, but who manifested a genuine commitment to Jesus Christ. They should be considered as much within the Church as Baptists. In the latter pamphlet, he said:

> There is no position in the whole compass of theology of the truth of which I feel a stronger persuasion, than that no man, or set of men, are entitled to prescribe as an indispensable condition of communion, what the New Testament has not enjoined as a condition of salvation.

Although Robert Hall was a Baptist by choice and conviction, he held to this broad and benevolent view to the end of his life. Interestingly, however, he could not go along with John Bunyan's concept of baptism. For Hall, baptism was for believers only. Nevertheless, he would not consider baptism a test for participation in the Lord's Supper.

William Carey was a friend of Robert Hall's. He was a staunch Baptist and founder of the modern missionary movement. As he matured in years and his faith deepened, he did not see how it would be possible to exclude non-Baptist Christians, such as Watts, Edwards, Brainerd, Dodderidge and Whitfield, from the Lord's Table and communion. Rather than engage in wild discussions about these kinds of

Popes, Pastors, and Presbyters

controversies over baptism, William Carey decided to keep a charitable spirit while holding firmly to his own views. He would allow his brothers to conscientiously profess their own convictions without withholding his love from them because of a minor doctrinal issue. It is obvious that Carey had a large view of life. He seemed able, in those early days of the Baptists, to see the whole world and the whole Church of Jesus Christ.

A more recent Baptist of note, Walter Rauschenbusch, at the turn of our century, is quoted by Sydnor Stealey's *A Baptist Treasury* as saying:

> I do not want to have Baptists shut themselves up in their little clamshells and be indifferent to the ocean outside of them. I am a Baptist, but I am more than a Baptist. All things are mine . . . because I am Christ's. The old Adam is a strict denominationalist; the new Adam is just a Christian.

Questions for Thought and Discussion

1. Is the form of your church's government important? Why or why not? If so, how important?
2. What similarities exist between the roles and responsibilities of the pastor and those of the nonordained men and women in a church? What differences are there?
3. What are the special qualifications and functions of a deacon?
4. What are the standards for ordination in your

church, and how does an individual become ordained?

5. What is the importance or meaning of baptism for an individual? What are some of the arguments used in support of various forms of baptism (immersion, sprinkling, and pouring)?

6. What is the religious meaning or significance of Communion for the participants? Why do you think different interpretations arose?

7. Should Communion be open to all believers or restricted to members of the local church? Why?

Suggestions for Further Study

Norman H. Maring, "Andrew Fuller's Doctrine of the Church," *Baptist Concepts of the Church,* op. cit., pp. 71-98.

10

A Freedom-Loving People

WHEN OUR LORD SAID, "Render unto Caesar the things that are Caesar's and unto God the things that are God's," He enunciated what Baptists have defined as "separation of church and state." He set forth the idea that church and state must occupy different areas of concern. This became a basic tenet of the early churches. For years following our Lord's statement, life moved ahead at its own leisurely pace and there was little confusion or conflict over this subject. But when the Roman emperor, Constantine the Great (306-337 A.D.), set out to consummate the merger of church and state, he set forces in motion that were to have serious consequences for later history. No sooner did Christianity become the religion of the state than persecution of minority groups began.

The Donatists, a group of dedicated Christians

and forerunners of the Anabaptist movement in the Middle Ages, resisted the secularization of the Church whereby it lost its character as a community of holy persons and was transformed into an institution of mixed character, "tares" and "wheat." They held that the Church of Jesus Christ must consist only of those who were converted and committed to their Lord. So they attempted to split away from the Church. In doing so they attracted dissident elements of society that hurt their cause. In the end they were forcibly squashed in a combined persecution by church and state. Of this period, historians have suggested that, for the first time, the ideas of Christianity, as opposed to the pagan religion of the state, became an object of contention within the state itself—the ideas concerning universal, inalienable human rights, liberty of conscience, and the right of free religious conviction. The struggle which began that day has continued for centuries in various countries, but the inherent longing of mankind for liberty of conscience has been universal.

When Gregory VII became supreme Pontiff of the Church (1073-1085) he laid the basis for a more radical union between church and state. He was an ambitious leader, conniving and maneuvering with counselors and parliaments, vying with kings for power. A case in point was Gregory's confrontations with Henry IV of Germany. Gregory and Henry were in conflict through most of Gregory's term. At one point, after being excommunicated, Henry was

A Freedom-Loving People

forced to stand with bare feet in the snow for a long period, in order to do penance. Ultimately, however, he was instrumental in having Gregory deposed.

As we have noted in earlier chapters, there were men within and without the church in these early centuries who, because they followed their consciences and God, were persecuted and even killed.

A new barrage of voices was raised during the Reformation. Freedom of conscience was one of the prime planks in their platform. Zwingli in Switzerland, Luther in Germany, Calvin in Switzerland and France, Knox in Scotland, and Wycliffe in England took up the cause of freedom. It is at this point we discover one of the strangest anomalies of history. Although the Reformers struggled for their own freedom, yet these great men used some of the same repressive tactics they decried in Romanism. Enigmatically, there is another side to these great men of faith and it is not a pleasant one. We see them persecuting, even as they had been persecuted. Luther turned against the God-fearing Anabaptists. Servetus was burned at the stake near Geneva and Melanchthon approved of the hideous act. Germany burned at the stake that mighty forerunner of the Baptists, Balthasar Hubmaier. Holland dispatched one of her finest statesmen, John of Barneveldt, and condemned one of her historians, Hugo Grotius, to life imprisonment—and all for conscience's sake. In England, Henry VIII burned Roman Catholics and Baptists at the same stake to authenticate his title,

THE BAPTIST HERITAGE

"the Defender of the Faith." Elizabeth renewed persecution in Smithfield for the same reason. James I was determined to break the spirit of nonconformity. Archbishop Laud, serving under Charles I, ruled the Church of England with fines, imprisonments, and tortures of all kinds—for example, cutting off ears, and branding scars upon the faces of his victims. Scottish Presbyterians interfered with the liberty of the press and civil power.

England kept John Bunyan, Baptist preacher, in prison for 12 years because he exercised his right to freedom of conscience in matters of the Christian faith. Helwys confronted his monarch with a withering denunciation of the king's extension of rule into the Baptists' private consciences. He was imprisoned and done away with for his impertinence.

The important thing to remember in this recitation of tragedy is that Baptists and their forerunners, then as now, were not attempting to be negative or obstructionist. Rather, they were affirming a very positive principle, the absolute Lordship of Jesus Christ and His control over the conscience of every man. In that light, any human interference must be judged as wrong because it becomes a usurpation of only God's prerogative. The Waldensian Confession of Faith, for example, states:

> We acknowledge that kings, princes and governors are the established ministers of God whom we are bound to obey. From this power and authority no

A Freedom-Loving People

one can exempt himself, as is manifest from the example of our Lord Jesus Christ Who voluntarily paid tribute, not taking upon Himself any jurisdiction of temporal power. By baptism we are received into the holy congregation of God's people, previously professing and declaring our faith and change of life.

The Baptist movement began, as we saw in Chapter One, with a small group of some 36 people who, with John Smyth and Thomas Helwys, sought refuge in Holland in order to escape the withering persecution of England's rulers. Freedom of conscience was so important to them that they uprooted their families, giving up their means of livelihood and security so as to freely exercise their consciences. In Amsterdam they formed the first Baptist church of which we have any knowledge. Later, under Thomas Helwys' leadership, they returned to London and formed the first Baptist church on English soil, at Spitalfield. Just prior to their return to England in 1611, these freedom-possessed people wrote what they called "A Declaration of Faith of English People Remaining at Amsterdam, Holland." This declaration stated that "no church ought to challenge any prerogative of any other church and the magistrate is not to meddle with religion, or matters of conscience, nor compel men to this or that form of religion." In so stating they affirmed both the autonomy or independence of the local church as well as the freedom of the individual conscience.

THE BAPTIST HERITAGE

The *Encyclopedia Britannica* says this was "the first known expression of absolute liberty of conscience in any confession of faith." These principles have been of great significance to Baptists from those days to the present.

In 1630, some ten years after the Pilgrims sailed, a young Welsh pastor sailed for America with his wife. Roger Williams would not budge on matters of conscience even though his life was in constant danger because of his stance. Banished from Massachusetts by the Puritans, ironically, for the same reason they had left England—freedom of conscience—he settled in Providence, Rhode Island. There he developed a new form of government among his fellowmen in which God would be supreme. There he established the first Baptist church on American soil. Individual consciences were to be acknowledged and respected. He secured a charter and on May 10, 1647, the first government since Constantine to declare the separation of church and state came into being in Rhode Island.

In Massachusetts, Obadiah Holmes was whipped on Boston Common for rejecting the state church and infant baptism. Clark and Croudell were imprisoned and heavily fined. In Connecticut, lands of Baptists were confiscated and sold to build a church. In Virginia Lewis Craig was imprisoned in Spotsylvania, William Webber in Chesterfield, John Shackleford in Essex—all because they preached the Gospel. Indians were forbidden to outwardly wor-

A Freedom-Loving People

ship their gods. Quakers were whipped, maimed, and banished. The President of Harvard University, because he was a Baptist, was convicted of heresy and forced to resign when he spoke against the state church.

In Virginia a child born of other than Episcopalians was considered illegitimate, and Baptist preachers were whipped and jailed. Everyone was taxed for the support of the Episcopalian Church. Patrick Henry, the great orator, became so involved in the Baptist cause in Virginia that he ascribed much of his philosophy of government and freedom to his association with them. Jefferson, a free-thinker, took up the Baptists' cause after studying their argument for freedom of conscience.

Baptists petitioned the First Continental Congress ever held in 1774 and "besought them to secure at once the recognition of the inalienable rights of conscience."

On and on the struggle went until complete liberty was declared and assured. These Baptists dared to defy traditions and customs and deliberately chose nonconformity even if it meant imprisonment or death. They pled, protested, agitated, and refused to keep silent until they had won to their side statesmen such as Washington, Jefferson, Madison and many others. Baptists did not effect religious liberty in this country by themselves, of course. There were many factors and influences. However, probably more than any other body or group of people, the Baptists

THE BAPTIST HERITAGE

played a major role in securing these guarantees of freedom.

Surely freedom is one of the most important considerations to man next to his own life. The First Amendment of our Constitution summarizes what separation of church and state meant to the 18th-century Baptists: "Congress shall make no law respecting an establishment of religion . . ." (i.e., no state church will be encouraged), and "Congress shall make no law . . . prohibiting the free exercise thereof [religion] . . ." (i.e., complete freedom of individual conscience).

Today, separation of church and state means exactly what it meant 200 years ago. The state cannot tell the church what to believe or what to preach. The church, in turn, does not seek funds from the state or influence to support its work.

By holding to this view of separation of church and state, Baptists have not meant to infer at any time that Christians should not be loyal citizens. Nor do they mean to preclude the presence of government-paid chaplains or tax exemptions for the church. Indeed, in many areas the church and state can work together, and do, for the betterment of mankind. In matters of the hungry, the destitute, or the homeless, our country has been in the vanguard of benevolent activity. And the church has worked with some government agencies to get food and clothing to needy areas of our world. For the church should be in the forefront of those helping to promote justice and

A Freedom-Loving People

equal opportunity for the disinherited and disenfranchised, and training programs for the down-and-out. These activities should not be mistaken for evangelism, but they are a godly response to human need. Yet, the separation between church and state in all of these activities is, nonetheless, maintained.

When Jesus told His contemporaries, "You will know the truth, and the truth will make you free" (Jn. 8:32, RSV), He was not addressing Himself to the problem of academic freedom or even political freedom. He was speaking about spiritual freedom, which was His gift to His followers. The freedom of Jesus Christ is the freedom from sin. He sought during His days on earth, even as He seeks today, to deliver men from bondage to self and to rid them of the things that imprison their spirits, such as legalism, superstition, lust, pride, or idolatry.

Paul the apostle picked up the theme and wrote: "Where the Spirit of the Lord is, there is liberty" (II Cor. 3:17). The apostle Peter exhorted his audience to live as free men without using their freedom as a pretext for evil (I Pet. 2:16). The apostle James preached about a "law of liberty" by which Christians were to act (Jas. 1:25).

While those who signed the Declaration of Independence showed respect for God and often quoted the Scriptures and ascribed what they called "self-evident truths" to the hand of the Almighty, their immediate concerns were not the theological aspects of freedom, but rather the matter of taxation without representation, political freedom for their citizenry, and economic independence. They were ready to die for these. So were the Baptists; but they had also added the spiritual dimension of freedom—freedom from sin through commitment to Christ.

Today, it is not enough to stress individual freedom or liberty of conscience. In an interlocking society individualism is not enough. Men are born alone, die alone, come to Christ alone; but our complex society forces mankind to live together. Baptists see that we must live our lives as a part of a human team, a world family that needs redeeming. Where there is hunger and destitution the church must seek to meet it head on. Where there is injustice, the church should follow Amos' example and point it out. Where there is corruption, the church should do everything it can to correct it. Where there is wanton waste, the church must practice and teach good stewardship of life and material. The Baptist will not take advantage of his neighbor merely because he has individual freedom. His freedom drives him to be his neighbor's brother.

Baptists have noted that where there has been tyranny, the Scriptures are considered volatile, inflammatory literature, and are banned. Queen Elizabeth I, for example, prohibited the Geneva Bible from coming into Britain because she knew that the Bible stirs the hearts of men; it forces them to think down to their center and creates dissatisfaction with dictatorial systems. The Bible excites a man's blood to freedom and justice. It produces in men a desire to become what they are potentially.

In 1773, Isaac Backus wrote, "An Appeal to the Public for Religious Liberty, Against the Oppressions of the Present Day." It was published in Boston. Backus commented:

> ... it appears to us that the true difference and exact limits between ecclesiastical and civil government is this, that the *CHURCH* is armed with light and truth, to pull down the strong holds of iniquity, and to gain souls to Christ, and into his church, to be governed by his rules therein; and again to exclude such from their communion, who will not be so governed; while the *STATE* is armed with the sword to guard the peace, and the civil rights of all persons and societies, and to punish those who violate the same. And where these two kinds of government, and the weapons which belong to them, are well distinguished, and improved according to the true nature and end of their institution, the effects are happy, and they do not at all interfere with each other; but where they have been confounded together, no tongue nor pen can fully describe the mischiefs that have ensued.

In this same document he says of the New England establishment that they sought very hard "to have the church govern the world, till they lost their charter; since which they have yielded to have the world govern the church."

Above any other contribution the Baptists have made to mankind has been their emphasis upon soul-liberty or freedom of conscience—liberty to believe, to respond to the Gospel directly, by the grace of God, with the responsibility that this places upon us all. "Brothers, we are children, not of a slave, but of One who is free. This is the freedom with which Christ has freed us. So stand firm in it, and do not get under the yoke of slavery again" (Gal. 4: 31; 5: 1, Goodspeed's American Translation).

Questions for Thought and Discussion

1. Upon what principle did the nonconformists base their struggle for freedom of conscience?
2. In what ways is an individual's freedom of conscience threatened today?
3. If you should find yourself in a situation where the freedom of your conscience is threatened, what should you do about it?
4. What political, social, and religious conditions mark the essential boundaries between the separation of church and state?
5. How does the presence of God's Spirit provide an individual with freedom and liberty?
6. Why must our Christian life today take us beyond the struggle for individual freedom?

Suggestions for Further Study

Torbet, *A History of the Baptists*, pp. 234-243.

PART III: Ministry

11

Evangelistic Involvement

IT WAS A TWO-AND-A-HALF HOUR FLIGHT from Rome to Cairo, and, as I boarded the plane, I realized how travel-weary I was. "God, please let me rest," I prayed. "Do not put anybody beside me on this leg of the journey because, frankly, I do not want to be bothered." God heard my prayer and left two seats next to me empty in an otherwise full airplane.

Midway through the flight, I looked up as the stewardess was pouring coffee and saw a pair of pretty but lonely eyes. Before I realized what I was doing I heard my voice saying, "What is your name?"

"Rosalind," came the reply.

"Rosalind, when you have a few moments, I would like to talk to you about something very special to me."

"I'll be back in a few minutes after I get my other stewardesses assigned," she said.

I went back to the book I had been reading, bemused and amazed at my effrontery and boldness. I heard a tiny voice inside me tauntingly ask, "All right, Big Mouth, what are you going to say to that stewardess when she comes back? Why didn't you think before you spoke?"

Soon, I heard her settling down into the seat next to mine. "Well, now, what did you want to talk to me about?" I was wondering the same thing! And I quickly breathed a silent prayer.

As we chatted about her hometown in Scandinavia, she told me about her family background in a Norwegian Lutheran church from which she had rebelled. She was now living, out of wedlock, with a pilot in Nice, France. She was lonely, feeling guilty and empty. I showed her some pictures of my lovely family and told her how my daughter, at nine years of age, had been watching a Billy Graham meeting on television. During the invitation hymn I had felt the davenport shaking. My daughter was crying, and she had asked me if she could invite Christ into her life, too. We prayed then and there, as thousands of others did that night, and my daughter became a daughter of God.

Rosalind listened to the story and her eyes sparkled with tears. I shared how, in my youth, Christ had taken away my emptiness and had given meaning to my life. I also recounted several other in-

Evangelistic Involvement

stances of how God had met my loneliness, and I sensed this was the focal point of our conversation. When Rosalind said, "Yes, I am terribly lonely, but how do I know Jesus Christ can do for me what you say?" I shared with her from memory several promises of our Lord from the Scriptures. I knew that we were descending into the Cairo Airport and that she must prepare for landing. So I asked her to go back to the restroom, and look into the mirror, and ask herself if she wanted to go on as she had been, or if she would "take God at His Word." When I disembarked, she grasped my hand, her face wreathed in smiles, and exclaimed softly: "Thank you, thank you, thank you!" I whispered the question: "Did you invite Christ into your life?" "Yes!" "Good, now read this little booklet." And I handed her a booklet that would clarify her decision through additional Scripture verses and diagrams.

D. T. Niles defined evangelism as "one beggar who has found bread showing another beggar where he too can find bread." Since we have feasted on the Bread of Life in Jesus Christ, surely we desire to share it with others. But it is important to remember that evangelism is not always reaping the harvest. It is not always helping people to come to Christ in one decisive moment, as Rosalind did. These are especially rewarding moments when a person receives Christ! But, for every person receiving Christ, we may speak to a dozen or more persons.

Now everything Christians attempt to do for

Christ is not evangelism, but certainly everything they do ought to be evangelistic. In other words, no person can be involved in a perpetual verbal presentation of the Gospel every moment of his life. Indeed, some Christians don't have the specific gift of making a verbal presentation of the Gospel with any degree of effectiveness. But it is axiomatic that a congregation of believers in a proper relationship to Jesus Christ finds evangelism taking place naturally in its relationship with the world around it. This is why it is somewhat artificial to make the separation between Baptist life-style in missions, on the one hand, and Baptist life-style in evangelism, Christian education and social concerns on the other; these overlap into a whole meaningful life-style. To minister or to serve, to be Christ's people, means to be involved in all of these. In doing the work of an evangelist, a missionary might, for example, feed and clothe his hungry friend (social concern) prior to sharing the Gospel in its specifics (evangelism) or teaching him the doctrines of the Scripture (Christian education), after which he may tend his illness or help find a solution to a tribal feud (social concern). One can readily see how there must be a definition of "mission" or "ministry" which includes all of these activities. In order to discuss and analyze them, however, we have separated these activities, but it is important to remember that they cannot be separated in practice without damaging one's life-style. We are not interested in formulating another

Evangelistic Involvement

plan for evangelism. There are enough of these about which volumes have already been written. We are concerned that we find God's strategy, focused in the life of Jesus Christ, the great Evangelist. God has laid down His plan in Scripture. Its application to changing societies is not as easily understood as the basics of His strategy, but even in its application our Lord has promised to guide us. One key point to remember is that we must never be bound by one method or technique. Each Christian has his own talents that contribute to the life of the Body. Each Christian is gifted by God's Spirit for specific areas of ministry (cf. Eph. 4, I Cor. 12)—though he may not yet be aware of this provision. He does not necessarily have to use the same methodology to achieve the one common goal of penetrating his society with Christ's Gospel.

It is significant that the metaphorical references of Jesus to Himself and His Body include salt, light, keys, bread, water and leaven. They all penetrate and permeate. Every believer must examine himself, as did our Baptist forebears, to see if he is helping to permeate society with Christ's Gospel, or if he is just a spectator watching others do their ministry. The natural habitat of the Church is out in the world.

In Ezekiel 47: 1-12 we are presented with a unique vision of the Church. The prophet sees water flowing from under the threshold of the Temple, out the eastern gate into the world. As the trickle moves silently into the world it grows deeper and wider. At

149

THE BAPTIST HERITAGE

last it is a veritable river. Wherever the water flows from this stream, new life results with fruit trees, flowers, fish, and every living creature abounding. The fruit will not fail because the source of its life comes from the sanctuary. Ezekiel sees the Church moving toward the world as the giver of life, hope and healing wherever it touches. The message is clear: the redemptive power of the Gospel is released as it moves from the sanctuary to the world.

Christians have felt sometimes that they needed to qualify for sainthood prior to beginning a ministry. But we only need to look at the characters of the Bible to realize that God can use anyone if he is available. After the flood, Noah found some ground in which to plant a vineyard. He took the fruit of the vine, produced wine, and took off on a wild drunk. Abraham, wanting to be assured of safety in Egypt, allowed his wife Sarah to be taken for a concubine to Pharaoh's court. Jacob connived with his mother to cheat his brother of his birthright. David committed adultery with Bathsheba, and then murdered her husband so that he could possess her as his own. Peter was stubborn and slow. Thomas was doubting. James and John wanted the highest place in the coming kingdom no matter what might happen to their fellow-disciples. The list could go on. Yet, the lesson is that God uses all kinds of people to do His bidding. In spite of our weaknesses, handicaps or evil backgrounds, God longs to use us. He specializes in our impossibilities!

Evangelistic Involvement

Perhaps, more than most denominations, the Baptists have stressed the Biblical role of the priesthood of believers and the individual responsibility for evangelism placed upon individual members of their fellowship. Each member of a Baptist church should be viewed as a minister. Paul the apostle wrote: "Lead a life worthy of the calling to which you have been called" (Eph. 4:1, RSV); "Take heed to the ministry which thou hast received in the Lord, that thou fulfil it" (Col. 4:17). The authority for this vision of ministry comes from Jesus Christ Himself: "I assure you that the man who believes in me will do the same things that I have done, yes, and he will do even greater things than these" (Jn. 14:12, Phillips); "Just as the Father sent me, so I am going to send you" (Jn. 20:21, Phillips).

Baptists have been a doggedly practical people, more prone to becoming little "technicians" for the Kingdom, pushing the right buttons at the right time, astutely awaiting the proper psychological moment, attending new seminars on evangelism, or participating in evangelism conferences, rather than "being evangelism" in their innermost being. For an evangelistic life-style necessitates being more than doing, because one's style-of-life is what one reflects of Jesus Christ as the result of being with Him. His attitudes become ours.

In recent years, some Baptists have shown the propensity for using the church as a protection against the realities of life, as though Jesus Christ died to protect the status quo or to ensconce us more thoroughly in our comfortable sanctuaries. This dangerous view has produced a syndrome that makes the local church central for the "really important activities" of ministry. The local church is made the repository of all worthwhile programming. The church's officers and members and building plans are all-important. Anything outside those narrow parameters poses a threat and is, functionally, viewed as hostile to the church. How far this is from Christ's example for the Church and from our forebears' vision! Enlightened Baptists disavow such attitudes and affirm their loyalty to the redeeming Gospel that makes every believer a minister, an evangelist, a disseminator of the Good News. Samuel Shoemaker, in his book *How to Become a Christian,* wrote: "The test of a man's conversion is whether he has enough Christianity to get it over to other people. If he hasn't there is something wrong with it."

It is out here in my secular society with all its evil, its death and vacuous, frantic activities-to-find-meaning, that the Church finds herself. This is what is meant when theologians say "God is not religious," or they refer to the "secularity of the Gospel." How true it is. The Gospel cannot be confined within the Church and still be Christ's Gospel.

Baptists have agitated, labored and suffered for this ideal. We have seen how in the early 17th century the established church of England was guilty

Evangelistic Involvement

of "putting God in a box," the dimensions of which were defined by the church and the ruling monarch. In essence, the Baptists were attempting to say that no church has the right to imprison God with its limited perspective, its programming, its cloistered view. God is the God of the universe. He sent His Son *not* to the Church, to be protected by her walls, her theology and her prelates, but to the world. In this sense, God is a worldly God and His Gospel is dealing with man's spiritual as well as secular needs. The arena of all this activity is not a lovely sanctuary, four-square, but the town's manufacturing plant, the grocery store, the bakery, the local hospital, the school, the streets, and the alleys of our cities and towns where people are being broken by sin and bound by spiritual blindness.

The church must be seen, not as a building, but as people, individually, assuming their ministry with responsible joy; daily, persistently, penetratingly, with a consistent life-style, becoming the extension of God's personality, God's smile, God's care. For the church is its members becoming the extension of God's hands, feet, mind and heart. The risen Christ lives in the midst of His people as they live-Him-out. They have Him as they give Him to others. They abundantly live as they extravagantly lose their lives to others. This is evangelism at its best. The world has too long seen the church dying in its traditional decency.

Every church member must allow God to make

THE BAPTIST HERITAGE

him a reincarnated Christ to his fellowman. If this is true, then people notice that there is a difference in the dimension and quality of the life being lived before them. There is no super-piety, no excessive self-consciousness, no phony mask; there is an end of game-playing, and religious role-assumption, and the mouthing of religious cliches about "the Book, the Blood and the Blessed Hope." A smarting relevance takes the place of an inane recitation of meaningless terms. Jesus becomes flesh again in His Body, the Church, reaching out to persons who need to be born again in every wonderful sense of that term. This is exciting! This is evangelism.

Evangelism is not optional. It is imperative for the Christian. It is God's method of reconciling the world to Himself. Jesus said: "What shall it profit a man if he gain the whole world and lose his own soul?" In that profound question we gain a growing sense of awareness of what a man's soul means to God.

After one has received his new life in Christ, by faith, how does he begin to be an evangelist? Pause and think about your family, friends and associates. Let your mind rove over that mental list. Allow God to put His finger, as it were, upon the name of one person for whom you can begin to pray. Pray that God will use your relationship, your caring, your sensitivity to meet his need, to love that person to Christ in the situation where you find him. "The earnest prayer of a righteous man has great power

Evangelistic Involvement

and wonderful results" (Jas. 5:16b, TLB). The very practical thing about prayer is that it enables you to love the person for whom you pray. Effective witnessing results from effective praying because effective praying produces caring love. It will also point up the areas in one's own life which might become a stumbling block to others. The Psalmist prayed: "Search me, O God, and know my heart: try me, and know my thoughts: And see if there be any wicked way in me, and lead me in the way everlasting" (Ps. 139:23, 24).

Most Christians seem to think that witnessing begins when they start to speak. Usually days, if not years, prior to the actual verbal presentation, one's witness has been present or absent in one's life-style and the way has either been prepared through relationship or walls have been built. This is what is meant when it is said that evangelism should be relational. One does not grab a friend, much less a stranger, by the lapels and ask, with dilated pupils, "My brother—are you saved?" Anyone doing that might receive a well-deserved rebuff couched in profane eloquence with an angry snarl asserting that he never was lost.

Need it be said? God is a gentleman. He is not rude nor does He employ rudeness or obtrusive tactics. Neither should His ambassadors. There is a sense in which the believer should have earned the right to speak to another person about his soul's relationship to God. Great tact and wisdom are necessary at this point. Zeal must be capped with a real empathy for the person's situation. The purpose of witness, predicated upon a life lived before and hopefully in a relationship with the person, is not to win points, to get a convert, or to turn the person around to our way of thinking. And surely it is not to make a Baptist out of him. Rather it is to relate to another human being the same love and concern that Jesus gave to those around Him. We literally share Christ with them. This is no time for argument or calculating traps. The Holy Spirit, in answer to earnest prayer, will let us know by an inner sense of "rightness" that we may now or may not now give our testimony to God's work in our own life. It is not uncommon to have knees knock, mouth dry up, and heart palpitate. However, we dare not become overly self-conscious. As God dealt with Moses, and asked him, after 40 years of isolation with his sheep on the back side of the desert, to go down to Pharaoh and say "Let my people go," so, He sends us forth. Moses remonstrated: "But . . . they will not believe me, nor hearken unto my voice . . . I am not eloquent . . . I am slow of speech, and of a slow tongue" (Ex. 4: 1-10). God knew that Moses was all of that and more, but He wanted Moses to go back to that sophisticated court of Pharaoh as His Ambassador. Moses, like us, failed to reckon with God. God said: "Go, and I will be with thy mouth, and teach thee what thou shalt say" (Ex. 4:12). That is God's promise to every believer who sets out to be an effective witness. One

Evangelistic Involvement

day, God will give him the appropriate words, if he does not rush out and try to manipulate the situation. It is good to want men saved. It is best to be available for God's use, like Moses, when God is ready. It is God who saves. There is no "plan of salvation" that saves. Even the Bible does not save. It is the task of the Savior to save through His Spirit, as we give faithful witness.

On one occasion, a well-known business executive in a small town was in need. I had lived my life-style before him on many occasions. He felt he knew me, and I him. His wife was leaving him because of his inordinate immorality. Then he had an ulcer burst, and he thought he would die. He asked to see me. In my eagerness to help him, I rushed to share the Gospel. His main need, at that moment, was my friendship, not my preachments. But I saw myself as the Good News bearer. I could almost hear the trumpets blast as I turned to the fray. Inadvertently, I pushed the Holy Spirit aside and with great zeal dove into the task of leading my friend to Christ. Hoping for any port in the storm, he dutifully went through my little ritual. I thought he had become a Christian. For weeks, I awaited a miraculous life change. There was none.

Sometime later, when the Olympic Track Team came to town for a banquet during an Olympic year, he was the Master of Ceremonies. He had asked me to give the invocation at the banquet. I arrived early to find that during the cocktail hour my new convert

THE BAPTIST HERITAGE

had become a roaring drunk. He staggered to the head table with red face and sat me down. He began his introduction: "Ladies and gentlemen (hic!). Here is a prince of a man who is going to bring the invocation (hic!). He's my pastor!" That did it! I almost crawled under the table. I heard God gently saying, "In your zeal to win this man you did not consult Me as to timing, his need, or my enablement. You cared about his conversion more than you cared about him as a person. So, here he is—your convert! He certainly is not one of Mine!" I learned a lesson that night I shall not forget.

How different was the approach to an elderly lady who had just come through exploratory surgery and was told there was no hope. Because I had related to her need over weeks and months in love and caring, the bad news prompted her to ask me to visit her. I responded. She was ready. She opened the conversation: "I am so happy you have come. You see, I am dying and I don't know how to die. I want to get ready." My heart melted for her. My inner man cried out "O God! Do not let me fail this dear woman in speaking forthrightly and simply to her need and help me to show her Your dear Son, who alone can give her forgiveness and the peace she wants to experience." God heard my prayer. One hour later, eyes filled with tears of thankfulness, she expressed her newfound faith to her daughter and said: "Oh! I feel so clean inside!" She had met God. Real evangelism had taken place.

Evangelistic Involvement

Questions for Thought and Discussion

1. How would you have answered Rosalind's question, "Yes, I am terribly lonely, but how do I know Jesus Christ can do for me what you say?"
2. How do you define "mission" or "ministry"?
3. What does the author mean when he says that everything we do ought to be evangelistic even if not everything we do is evangelism?
4. What are the essential qualities that a person must have in order to be used by God in evangelism?
5. Why is the "natural habitat" of the Church out in the world?
6. Why is evangelism an imperative for a Christian rather than an option?
7. What does the author mean when he says "evangelism should be relational"? Why is this concept important?

Suggestions for Further Study

Torbet, *A History of the Baptists*, pp. 299-305.

12

Missionary Outreach

BAPTISTS ARE PEOPLE who believe that the Gospel is not a private possession but something to be shared with the world under the orders of Christ's Great Commission, "Go ye into all the world." God's heart is essentially a missionary heart, "For God so loved the world, that he gave his only begotten Son, that whosoever believeth in him should not perish, but have everlasting life" (Jn. 3:16).

Since by virtue of our faith in Christ we have become united with Him, His death has become our death, His life our life, His place our place, His wealth our wealth, and His work our work. There is but one task before us: the world's evangelization. Because we have admitted Christ into our lives, submitted our wills to His will, and committed our interests to His care, we must now transmit His Gospel to others. We are the medium of transmission. Two significant words in the Christian move-

Missionary Outreach

ment are *come* to Jesus, and *go* into all the world. There is also the valid principle: "What you don't use you lose." We must either share our faith or, in a very real sense, begin to lose it. Keeping it alive in its freshness, warmth and vitality depends upon our giving it away to others. This faith does not consist of a list of right words or a prescribed plan of salvation, but a permanent part of our life-style in which the Good News makes us Good News people. Christ's loving-kindness leaps out of us. His sensitivity to people's hurts and needs becomes our sensitivity as He uses our hands, feet and purses as His own for the all-important endeavor of disseminating His truth to those who need to hear it.

The Christian Gospel often has been suppressed by governments and monarchs, but it always has emerged again as men have become involved in the excitement and responsibility of liberty and freedom of conscience. Baptists, in the vanguard of that quest, have never viewed freedom of conscience as a private possession, but, of necessity, as something that must be shared with all men everywhere. Baptist movement pioneers never attempted to force the world to their way of belief, but they simply accepted the right to think for themselves and to freely worship God because they regarded this as vital for everyone.

The Wesleyan revival had a marked influence upon life in England. Strangely, English Baptists, who fell into two groups—the General Baptists

THE BAPTIST HERITAGE

(Arminians) and the Particular Baptists (Calvinists)—did not participate in the movement at the beginning. They were suspicious of Wesley because of his advocacy of infant baptism and his Arminian views. Even though George Whitefield was a Calvinist, the Particular Baptists of England rejected him because he gave open invitations to receive Christ. Hyper-Calvinistic, they believed only a select few could be saved. Since God had already chosen those who would comprise His Kingdom, they contended that no evangelist should engage in aiding God where such aid was not requested. This hyper-Calvinism had a weakening effect upon the Particular Baptists, who felt no compunctions to evangelize; in fact, to send missionaries to foreign fields was unthinkable. Many of their pastors were so antipathetic to Arminianism that they would not give an invitation to the unconverted, feeling that to do so would rob God of the sole glory of converting the lost. Sydnor L. Stealey's *A Baptist Treasury* cites one of the leading Particular Baptists of that time, John Gill:

> Election is of particular persons; it does not merely respect events, characters, and actions; but the persons of men; as they are persons who are chosen in Christ, and appointed, not to wrath, but to obtain salvation by him; so there are persons who are foreordained to condemnation, whose names are left out of the book of life, whilst others are written in it.

Missionary Outreach

Stemming from such views was a feeling of futility regarding the unsaved. The established church could do absolutely nothing for them. It was no one's duty to lead them to repentance, faith or prayer, because these were considered divine gifts of grace and not human achievement. To the hyper-Calvinist, Christ died not for the whole world but for the elect alone.

One of William Carey's biographers, S. Pearce Carey, suggests:

> The pulpit doctrine of his [Carey's Baptist] denomination was extravangantly predestinarian. God's sovereignty was stressed till our responsibilities vanished. Man was declared to have no power for penitence or faith, save through the super-enabling of God's selective grace. Here was no driving force for Missions. Faith ossified into fatalism. With the occult divine Will omnipotent and the human will judged helpless, even the godly grew passive. They who could think themselves the privileged exulted in their fortune, but remained unconscious of owing the good tidings to others. The favour was for the few. They left to God the ingathering of His own selected guests.

William Carey had sat under the ministry of Robert Hall, Sr. (1728-1791), who preached a sermon in the Northamptonshire Association that was like a bomb blast, published in 1781 under the title, *Help to Zion's Traveller*. This booklet sought to alleviate some of the problems and tensions regarding salvation's universal availability in contradistinction to limited salvation. Hall's preaching opened some cracks in the impenetrable wall dividing England's Baptists. Based on his theological development of grace for all men, he urged preachers to extend an invitation to the lost. Carey openly supported this view, as did other eager protagonists like John Ryland, Robert Hall, Jr., John Sutcliff, Samuel Pearce and Andrew Fuller.

Fuller played an essential role in founding the first missionary society, which sent Carey to India. Its first secretary, he worked arduously for worldwide missions, raising large sums of money by traveling throughout the country. From 1792 until his death in 1815, he was easily the most relevant thinker and eloquent voice for missions in the world. His secretarial services were enormous. As a writer and scholar helping to shape Christian thinking during this controversy, he was skilled, convincing and Spirit-filled.

The missionary spirit among American Baptists began to grow during the first half of the 19th century, with Fuller's theology as a main contributing factor. Others were Carey in India, Adoniram and Ann Judson in Burma, Luther Rice in America (who was sponsored by the 1814 Triennial Convention of Philadelphia). From then on Baptists were notably and passionately missionary in their life-style. Today each major Baptist denomination has hun-

Missionary Outreach

dreds of missionaries scattered abroad. The saga of their manifold exploits for Christ in spreading the Gospel has never been fully told. Fuller's and Carey's theology, emphasizing the availability of Christ's grace and forgiveness for everyone, succeeded precisely because it was Biblical and had God's blessing upon it.

The modern missionary enterprise calls for every Christ-honoring person to help through prayer, finances, and the giving of sons and daughters to the work of evangelism, education, healing, and training in the numerous skills of construction, education, agriculture, and medicine. Some countries have needed more specific kinds of expertise than others. Missionaries have entered difficult situations, not out of a desire to "Americanize" or "colonize," but to literally work themselves out of their jobs by preparing indigenous leaders to take over their work and perhaps send missionaries to others one day. The fruit of this missionary philosophy was seen when Baptists were forced to leave Burma, and it will occur again as pressures continue to rise in other countries for Yankees to go home. Trained, dedicated persons are being left behind to continue the work. It is being done well, both in terms of preparing these peoples and then allowing them to take over over the reins of the work.

It is obvious that the scope of missionary endeavor has come to embrace more of the material needs of all peoples, their health, their housing, and those things that make for a deeper sense of personal worth under God, as well as proclaiming the important Christian doctrines. Surely, in light of the world's millions of starving people, we must ask ourselves, "Are we willing to live less well and to accept greater tax burdens so that people in other countries may have a more equitable opportunity to survive and learn how to help themselves?" To those who might say, "This is not within the province of missions or the Church's ministry," we can only answer, "That seems to be a grossly inadequate response."

When Christ's Church goes into all the world, it is unable to stop with making people Christians. Indeed, might it not be evil to offer Christ to a starving man unless we have first offered him food? Will he not be better able to understand the Gospel message as Good News if he has tasted of the literal good news of food for an empty stomach? Equally, might it not be evil to offer bread to a well-fed man until we have first offered him the saving Gospel? In such instances, our food might become a stumbling block or a blessing. Somehow the Word of God has a way of stimulating a desire in the underprivileged for better economic advantages. This is usually evidenced wherever the Gospel has gone. By improving sanitation, by assisting people to eradicate intestinal worms through personal hygiene, by teaching nutrition and the proper tending of newly born babies, and by medical aid we demonstrate the Gospel.

Missionary Outreach

Regarding such activity, some would ask, "How long can the 'have' countries attempt to feed and clothe the 'have not' countries? Are we not courting bankruptcy, if not adding to the indigenous problem, by creating more mouths to feed?" A counterreply could be that, quite realistically, we might be dragged down to the low economic condition of the rest of the world by the cost of military armaments to protect ourselves from the "have nots" unless we attempt to lift them up to our level. In light of the ever-enlarging number of nations joining the "nuclear club" and the recent development of relatively low-cost methods of preparing nuclear bombs, we might find ourselves in a position of susceptibility to international blackmail unless we do what we feel Christ would have us do. Although we are not qualified to judge such weighty matters that need answers from informed experts, yet we have the uneasy feeling that perhaps they, with us, are sailing on an uncharted course in such matters.

For some, a "safe" position is to accept Christ's Great Commission and go into the world preaching, teaching and healing in His name and leave the outcome to Him. If our Lord were discussing this matter with His Church, what would He say? Surely He wants us to ponder these things and seek His counsel before we proceed.

These are difficult days for world missions with doors closing upon missionary enterprise in numerous places and with the cry of isolationism from many quarters. For times like these, it helps to remember that the Baptist missionary movement in its early days looked bleak when Adoniram Judson, after seven years of suffering and abuse, had but one convert to show for his labor in Burma. The movement that had been given impetus by the great vision and faith of William Carey and Andrew Fuller could not, at that time, be called a success. David Livingstone, with one arm hanging useless at his side and with illness throughout his body, came to his life's end with little to show for his sacrifice in Africa. Who can forget Robert Morrison, who died without realizing his dream of ever having found entrance to the main gate of China? Then there was Roger Williams, who was banished from Massachusetts Bay, an unwanted pest in the eyes of the magistrates and most of his peers. Yet, all these men showed confidence in God's purpose and plans, for they could see beyond the circumstances of their local situation. "The light still shines in the darkness and the darkness has never put it out" (Jn. 1:5, Phillips).

Virtually all Christians have relished the story in Jeremiah 32 of a faith that is as audacious as that which modern missions must exemplify if we are to be equipped for these days of worldwide witness.

The scene was Jerusalem during the seige by the Babylonian army. The prophet Jeremiah had been imprisoned in the royal palace dungeon because he had repeatedly prophesied the city's fall and the

Missionary Outreach

captivity of King Zedekiah, who did not like his negativism. Hunger within the city was so severe that some mothers were purported to have eaten their own children. At the height of the disheartenment and portending doom, Jeremiah's cousin visited the prophet to tell him of a piece of family land that was evidently at or near the site occupied by the Babylonian army. The property was for sale, and Jeremiah was entitled to the first right to buy it. Jeremiah knew where the land was located, and he also knew that God had said Jerusalem would fall to Nebuchadnezzar. The land would be taken, along with the Israelites and King Zedekiah. However, Jeremiah also knew that God was not finished with Israel. There would be a new day, perhaps years hence, when that piece of land, now worthless, would be valuable. So, based upon his heroic trust in God, with all outward evidence showing him to be a poor, self-blinded purchaser of worthless land, he meted out the silver required for the full purchase price. He filled out the documents before witnesses and announced publicly, before prison guards and witnesses, his prophecy about the city's fall. But he added God's new revelation that the city would one day be reborn and the land would have new value. God would manifoldly restore the land purchased. God's Covenant with Israel would remain.

The hard days of the missionary movement's beginnings in England, India, Burma and America were almost enough to shake the faith of the most

THE BAPTIST HERITAGE

faithful saints. Yet, like Jeremiah, they kept the faith, persistently looking to the problem-solver, Almighty God, rather than dwelling upon the problems that threatened them and instead of pawing through the rubble of circumstances.

They passed on a legacy of faith and hope to the following generations as millions came into the Kingdom of God through missionary efforts.

Recently I visited Kialu in the backwoods of Zaire, Africa, on a Sunday morning. Several thousand Zaireans jammed a building built for one-third that number. After an unforgettable baptism of 186 people in the river, the barefooted throngs walked back to the Kialu church, singing as they went, with the aid of rattles and drums and other strange-sounding instruments. An announcement was made that the offering was to be received. To our amazement, a pan big enough to hold at least four babies for a bath was passed over their heads as people threw in their coins or *makutu*. This sight was strange and intriguing as these Baptists joyfully gave their money. Obviously, from seeing their school, medical center and outreach ministries, they had also given their lives. The purpose of the offering caught us by surprise. The pastor announced that there was a struggling sister church in the Philippines, "halfway around the world from here, and we want to send a love offering to help in their work." Suddenly, the work to which I had given in Africa was passing on its blessings to yet another church in need that its

Missionary Outreach

members would probably never see in their lifetime. In joyfulness, the Body of Christ in Kialu participated in this missionary outreach for another part of Christ's Body 10,000 miles away.

Another form of missionary activity has been developing among the numerous international students studying in American universities. These young people complete their education and return to their homelands, often as government leaders, and make a great impact upon their own people. Contacts are easily secured through the universities when the nature of the church's interest is understood. An invitation is sent to the hundreds of students in an area to visit a local church or to attend an international student's banquet with a mixture of cultures and religions. Their loneliness and curiosity draw them. Food is provided for vegetarians or those with other dietary requirements, and warm friendship is shared, along with a program in which the arts, crafts, and music of several cultures are demonstrated. Christian witness is given through the fellowship and the message by an outstanding Christian international. Field trips and social and recreational activities are provided to broaden the students' understanding of America. Sometimes practical needs are met, such as those of a Muslim couple about to have their first child. They were worried where they would find baby clothes and other necessary items. Local church women made a layette and provided more than was needed. Tears of joy were followed by the

THE BAPTIST HERITAGE

exclamation, "But we are Muslims! Why should Christians care for Muslims?" They were assured that having a baby is exactly the same for Muslims or Christians, and that out of love and concern the women counted it a privilege to share with their Muslim friends. The word spread rapidly through hundreds of internationals: "If you are lonely or in need, be sure to go to that church. There you will find love." That is local evangelism and missions. Perhaps that couple will never profess faith in Christ, but they have felt the impact of His love. They could never return home without a wholesome remembrance of Christians.

Agricultural missionaries have gone to the hill tribes of Thailand to help them triple their economy and enhance their diet with fish from newly constructed fishponds. Crop rotation and special seed that grows better rice or corn opens doors to a better life as well as to the Gospel. Meet the economic needs, and you discover a warm invitation to share the Good News.

To alleviate the heavy opium traffic in the Karen Hills, two Baptist missionaries have gone into dangerous situations where the opium poppy is grown openly. To attempt to stop the farmers from their lucrative means of living would bring grave danger, if not death. Yet, with government and church support, new and more lucrative crops have been substituted. By this divine sublimation, not only are the tribesmen better off financially, but such

Missionary Outreach

results bring joy and trust in their hearts for the missionaries who are showing them how it is done. Inevitably, opportunities are plenteous to present the Gospel in that context, and national evangelists and Bible teachers take over as the missionaries leave for another location.

Thus, Baptists have eagerly lived out their missionary life-style wherever they have gone. They have been concerned about the total person, including his environment, health and education as well as his soul. Their concern is not to usurp the right and dignity of the people to be themselves culturally, but to allow them to form their own style of worship and outreach along the guidelines of Holy Scripture. Leadership is placed in the hands of the local church after providing sufficient training. Seeking to work themselves out of a job does not mean abandonment of the work begun by missionaries. Rather, it means transferring leadership from foreign hands into local hands. The missionary works alongside as a resource person who seeks to be an enabler and an asset rather than a paternalistic "God-father" and liability. Growth in Christ is the all-important goal.

It is significant, as one searches I Corinthians 15, to find the words: "Christ died for our sins . . . He was buried . . . He appeared" (vss. 3-5, NASB). Each of these verbs is in the aorist tense, showing once-for-all action, completed in the past. However, the verb "rose" (vss. 4, 12) is in the perfect tense, signifying action that was begun in the past but

THE BAPTIST HERITAGE

which is still continuing. Christ's resurrection has brought our Savior and Lord into our present arena of life. He lives among His people. We can hear Him in the laugh of a child or see Him in the tears of a refugee or peering out of the clouded eyes of an old man. Christ meets His Church wherever it keeps its eyes open and trusts in His promises. The open eye is the eye that weeps today, but it is also the eye that smiles and celebrates God's working in the midst of man's muddle. Baptists, who have had the joy of being a significant part of Christ's worldwide missionary activity, were called under God to be the founders of the first missionary society. Not only have they perpetuated the labors of Carey, Judson and Rice, but they also have reflected in their lifestyle the great missionary heart of the living God who "so loved the world, that he gave his only begotten Son," the world's first Missionary.

Questions for Thought and Discussion

1. Do you agree with the author that, "We must either share our faith or, in a very real sense, begin to lose it"? Why?
2. How can we avoid the error of overemphasizing one doctrine (as the hyper-Calvinists did) to the detriment of our total Christian life?
3. What impresses you most about the lives of missionaries you have known or read about?
4. Why is it important to feed the hungry and heal the

sick as well as preach the Gospel to them? Can you find a Biblical basis for your answer?

5. Is it part of our Christian commitment to upgrade the life-style of surrounding poorer countries—even if that means lowering our own standard of living?

6. Read Jeremiah 25. What is its message for modern missions?

Suggestions for Further Study

Torbet, *A History of the Baptists,* pp. 331-355, 385-410.

13

Christian Education

BAPTISTS, A PEOPLE of evangelism and missionary outreach, likewise give high priority to Christian education, the continuing process by which the learner enters into a changed Christian behavior through guided experiences. Christian education is the process used to *learn* God's will, *grow* in grace, and *change* into new persons in Christ. These are the essential objectives of education: learning, growing, changing.

When Jesus was on earth, the synagogue school served as the center for religious education. Renowned scholars were the products of these schools. For centuries after Christ, the Christian faith was taught in monastic schools related to Roman Catholicism, or in Protestant homes and universities. Their methodology is considered antiquated today, but it had its effect as teachers established a

Christian Education

catechism, a series of questions for which they had composed written answers. The children learned to parrot back the correct answers.

Among the earliest catechisms was the one drafted by Martin Luther and used widely throughout Germany. The Presbyterians of England compiled the Westminster Catechism, which the Puritans accepted. The Particular or Calvinistic Baptists wrote their own catechism, basing it upon the Westminster Catechism but making alterations at the point of baptism. Later in America, the Philadelphia Association adopted this English Baptist Catechism as the norm for Baptists in America. Finally completed in 1742, it was named the Philadelphia Confession. John Calvin's views were predominant with strong emphasis upon God's sovereignty over mankind and man's corresponding inability to attain salvation apart from the Holy Spirit's work in his heart.

In time, some Baptists in early America felt the Philadelphia Confession was too extreme. In New England in 1780, Benjamin Randall organized a group called the Freewill Baptists who provided an option to the strong Calvinism of the day. By 1833 some Calvinistic Baptists in New Hampshire wrote the New Hampshire Confession of Faith, which was much less Calvinistic than the Philadelphia Confession. These were the two greatest confessional documents to affect early Baptists in America.

These creeds or confessions were ostensibly meant to provide norms or standards of the Christian

THE BAPTIST HERITAGE

faith to be passed down to future generations as summary statements of belief. They were never used as a test of doctrinal purity, nor were they binding upon a person's conscience, but they were revered guidelines of doctrine meant to be helpful and not doctrinaire.

The first Sunday school's origin is unknown as to the date of founding or meeting place. In 1780 Robert Raikes, a publisher, printer and layman of Gloucester, England, was saddened by the condition of thousands of children. An unbelievable number were delinquent ragamuffins, some without parents, and all overworked and abused. Raikes determined to do something about the problem. His venture began with four paid teachers and a five-hour session from 10 a. m. to 12 noon and from 1 to 4 p. m. on Sundays, the only free time many children had from their work at the factories. Soon these "Sunday schools" were emerging throughout England and spreading to the American colonies. Probably some of the colonies had Bible teaching for children during Sunday afternoons, but there is no substantiating historical documentation. Suffice it to say, the Sunday school movement caught on in America and spread like wildfire. With the Bible as the textbook, the teacher employed his best talents to make the Scriptures palatable to the children. In many classes, adults and children sat side by side, for graded classes and Sunday school literature had not yet been developed. The need to bring together ideas and

Christian Education

working principles was seen by Sunday school leaders during America's rapid development in the 19th century. In 1824 the American Sunday School Union was formed, which aided in bringing together the many Sunday schools already operating as well as helping to start many new schools. Not only did established churches begin to have Sunday schools, but many churches were born out of Sunday schools.

On February 25, 1824, the Baptist General Tract Society was established. At first it printed numerous Gospel tracts and booklets. By 1840 it was involved in book publishing, which has continued until today. Its current name is the Board of Educational Ministries and Publication of the American Baptist Churches. It also publishes other Christian materials now.

The Southern Baptist Convention created its Sunday School Board in 1891, entrusting to it the publication of all necessary materials to further the Southern churches' educational program. Since then, these and other publishing companies of the various Baptist bodies have produced millions of quarterlies, periodicals for graded classes, and teachers' helps.

Because some local Baptist churches did not always accept the views or the emphases of their denominational literature, they turned selectively to independent publishers of Sunday school literature. On occasion, denominational publishers decried the dangers of "a lack of continuity" in the casual unorganized approach of some churches. Yet, Baptists have historically chosen their own literature as they saw the need, denomination or no. Among the best known independent publishing houses for Gospel literature are David C. Cook Publishing Co., Scripture Press, and Gospel Light Publications. Competition obviously has had an impact both in the quality and motivation for all publishing houses to upgrade their materials. Baptist productions have notably improved over the years, as have the products of the independent publishers. Competition has actually aided the overall production and the results for Christ.

In any Baptist philosophy of education, there is a notable difference from most hierarchical churches. The focus has been upon the individual, with all educational programs designed to protect and enhance him in his own right of decision. The purpose of Christian education has never been to teach pupils how to gather data, for data-gathering is not good education. Instead, Baptists have sought for personal behavior changes in the direction of being like Jesus Christ. Anything short of that has not been considered a worthy goal. Naturally data is important, and Baptists clearly do not demean facts and information, but they believe that to educate by merely passing on dates, names, and places, or by memorizing names of the books of the Bible without any pertinence to the student's life situation, is unthinkable. Data must be shared in such dynamic contexts and need-resolving ways as to be assimi-

Christian Education

lated readily and eagerly in the process of an experience that is changing one's behavior patterns to be more Christ-like. This is specifically why Baptists have rejected catechisms in recent generations. Rote parroting of data is meaningless if there is no life situation to back it up. To paraphrase Christ's words: "What shall it profit a pupil if he has memorized all the books of the Bible and knows all the kings of the Old Testament, and can draw all of Paul's missionary journeys on a chart, if he loses his own soul!"

Advanced Sunday school literature must stress experience-centered activities so that learning takes place in a "doing" context, particularly a need-resolving context. Thus, methodology involves guiding, developing, showing, involving, and sharing with pupils. Caution must be taken at the point where education erodes to the mere dissemination of facts rather than the involvement of people in life-changing experiences with those facts; perhaps words are fluent and the teacher is impressed with his own thoroughness, yet the pupil has learned nothing. This is vacuous verbalism. A teacher needs to be careful at the point of misreading a pupil's apparent interest and his real understanding.

Do teachers rely on such extrinsic motivation as prizes, buttons, candy, field trips, gold stars, or threats to keep people coming, or do they structure the lesson experience around the known needs and the readiness of the pupils in order to resolve those needs, resulting in a delightful teaching experience with minimal discipline problems? The latter method is intrinsically motivated teaching. The lesson is itself so rewarding that learning takes place without pressure, leverage or manipulation.

The aim of Baptist Sunday schools is to have a Christ-centered program to honor Him, to proclaim His Gospel, and to train people in the applicable truths of Holy Scripture as they relate to their lives.

The approach of Sunday schools is pupil-centered, without apology. The concern is not so much with facts and information or even the physical properties with which one is working, but with persons, whole persons who need to know more about living for Christ in a difficult, strife-ridden world. Everything that is done will take into consideration that all-important pupil.

The content of Sunday schools is Bible-centered. Literature is selected by such criteria as: (1) Is it Biblically sound, Christ-centered, and Gospel-oriented? (2) Is it graded to the particular age group for which it is intended? (3) Is it structured for the changing of persons, and does it provide evidence that the authors have established goals and objectives which give hope for the realization of those goals? (4) Is it psychologically sound? Is it dealing with felt needs and problems where people are? Is it up-to-date in its developmental understanding of the pupils? (5) Is it showing that it is concerned about the average Sunday school teacher's ability or lack of ability to teach? Are there sufficient helps?

Christian Education

The method of Sunday schools should be experience-centered. The pupil will allow information to run off his back like water unless he is involved in the excitement of experiencing something that meets him at the point of his present needs. This is a difficult assignment for even seasoned teachers. How does one design a lesson plan that will meet the needs of all the pupils and achieve the desired behavior changes? Good Sunday schools never cease working at this problem, and good literature helps the teachers to face it.

The organization of Sunday schools is church-centered. The Sunday school does not run off and do its own thing, for it is an integral part of the church and not its competitor. By design and administration, the Sunday school must fit harmoniously into the total church program and accept its assigned sacred role with joy. It should support the church and never fight with it, bringing joy and not worry to the pastor and church officers. Its purpose is to feed and prepare people for the minister's message, not to provide a battleground for teachers to challenge the church's message.

It will utilize every helpful technique known to man to capture attention, to meet human need, and to ground persons experientially in the Word of God and the truths of the Gospel. This will be accomplished by employing visual aids, group discussions, quizzes, round-table discussions, forums, debates, role playing, drama, and field trips. There will

THE BAPTIST HERITAGE

be lectures (discovering), communication (telling), construction (making), skills developed (proficiency), and fellowship (enjoying fellow believers).

As a vital part of their concern for Christian education, Baptists have developed universities and theological seminaries. The first president of Harvard College was Henry Dunster, who by his scholarship, enthusiasm and professional competency led Harvard to a level of higher education before being fired from his position during those difficult colonial years because of his Baptist views. Yet, Harvard was founded in 1636 so as "not to leave an illiterate ministry to the churches, when the present ministers shall lie in the dust."

Brown University, founded in 1764 as Rhode Island College, was the first Baptist college in the colonies, with its purpose to be "securing for the church an educated ministry."

The first theological seminary was begun in 1817 to fill the need for pastors to have greater proficiency in the Scriptures and theology. Seminary students took a three-year course after four years of college, with Bible history, Church history, plus the skills of interpretation, communication and theology as the principal subjects.

While evangelism primarily emphasizes reaching the lost, this involves missionary outreach as well as teaching converts. Likewise, Christian education frequently finds converts through teaching as it becomes involved in social concerns when the students live out their lessons by caring for others or participating in projects. Thus, evangelism, missionary outreach, Christian education and social concern are intertwined.

Questions for Thought and Discussion

1. What standards of the Christian faith today function as guides to the teaching and understanding of its doctrines?
2. In your opinion, what is the main purpose of Christian education?
3. How does an awareness of the difference between intrinsic and extrinsic motivation apply to Christian education?
4. What are the greatest needs or problems facing Sunday schools and programs of Christian education today?
5. How can these needs or problems be met?

Suggestions for Further Study

Torbet, *A History of the Baptists,* pp. 305-330, 445-450.

14

Social Ministry

FROM THEIR REFORMATION ROOTS through the early English and American beginnings of their movement, Baptists were agitating, storming the walls of government totalitarianism, and demanding freedom of conscience and civil liberties for all people. So energetic were their efforts—even to leaving homes or country and enduring the privations of suffering and prison—that some might mistakenly believe that the Baptists' origin stems from the furor engendered by their social concerns rather than from their spiritual concern. Yet, history has shown that the spiritual principles so important to Baptists have been the motivating force causing them to regard social service as being integrally united with the genuinely Christian life-style.

Christ sent His followers to people to witness, to heal, and to offer themselves to them. If in living out their life-style they were called upon to suffer for

Social Ministry

their faith, they were to suffer on behalf of people. They were to follow in the train of the Savior who did not die for a plan of salvation or an establishment or organization or even for truth, but for people.

So it has been an imperative for most Baptists in their relatively brief history to be involved with people at the levels of their hurting as they have sought to uplift, to change life's circumstances, even as they pressed the claims of Christ for individual salvation. Blending evangelism and social service has been a hallmark of Baptists from their beginnings. This is not to say that there have been no exceptions, for some Baptists have seen their role solely in the context of saving souls, while others have viewed their task as the redemption of society's ills. Theological discussions have been numerous and, at times, heated. Dissension has accrued due to the differences of opinion concerning the mission of the Church. Yet, the rank and file of the Baptists have accepted, at least in theory if not always in practice, that Jesus Christ came to die for the whole world in its whole setting and that seeking individual salvation without social change, where people are being dehumanized and debilitated, would be less than Christian.

C. S. Lewis' classic *Screwtape Letters* has Screwtape writing a hurried note to Wormwood from hell about one of their former patrons who, in his view, had stupidly and blindly slipped into union with the Church. The Senior Devil says that he should not be downhearted. Rather, this should give Wormwood the opportunity of a new tactic, namely, "to keep the patron's mind on the inner life . . . keep his mind off the most elementary duties by directing it to the most advanced and spiritual ones. Aggravate that most useful human characteristic, the horror and neglect of the obvious."

In every branch of the Christian faith there is this blighting tendency to neglect the obvious in the interest of mouthing shibboleths and spiritual test words for the orthodoxy of the faith. For some it is apparently easier to love "souls" while hating people, as enigmatic as that might seem. Still others find they are possessed with social causes while having little concern for individual persons. Karl Barth's *Community, State and Church* suggests, "This Gospel which proclaims the King and the Kingdom . . . is political from the very outset, and if it is preached to real . . . men . . . it will necessarily be prophetically political." Then Barth suggests that if this political dimension of the Gospel is not an historical reality how can Christianity be salt or light and penetrate its society? The nature of true Christianity is to penetrate its milieu. On occasions this penetration assumes political, financial, ethical, moral or spiritual dimensions. Barth seems to be suggesting that there is no easy bifurcation or separation of meeting human need at a spiritual level, and at the same time ignoring the other levels that affect man's total life.

Social Ministry

Baptists have exemplified the conviction that when a man accepts the Christian faith he must not shirk responsibility to his society but should seek new concern and commitment to it, finding his place in the tradition of the prophets and the apostles. As he studies Scripture, he finds his role is not in some special, removed, monastic sphere of life but within life's mainstream. He is expected to become involved, to assume his ministry no matter how he makes his living. He learns, like Israel wandering in the wilderness or at Sinai, that, while there is a difference between the sacred and the profane, there is an integral relationship between the social and the spiritual. When God sees social wrong He sees moral wrong. The Ten Commandments (Ex. 20) became a unique codification of God's mind for the social context of man's life.

In Israel's world a deadening cynicism and indifference to human life was eroding civilization. In the middle of this kind of world, prophets were thundering, "Thus saith the Lord!" The Old Testament laws were not written to a trouble-free society but to a society struggling to find its human community. God was deeply concerned about the social and community life of His people, even as He is today. Read Psalm 146 and sense God's concern for the societal issues:

But happy is the man who has the God of Jacob as his helper, whose hope is in the Lord his God—the

THE BAPTIST HERITAGE

> God who made both earth and heaven, the seas and everything in them. He is the God who keeps every promise, and gives justice to the poor and oppressed, and food to the hungry. He frees the prisoners, and opens the eyes of the blind; he lifts the burdens from those bent down beneath their loads. For the Lord loves good men. He protects the immigrants, and cares for the orphans and widows. But he turns topsy-turvy the plans of the wicked (TLB).

The prophet Micah declared God's concern for social justice and compassion when he said:

> Will the Lord be pleased with thousands of rams, or with ten thousands of rivers of oil? shall I give my firstborn for my transgression, the fruit of my body for the sin of my soul? He hath shewed thee, O man, what is good; and what doth the Lord require of thee, but to do justly, and to love mercy, and to walk humbly with thy God? (Micah 6:7, 8).

The prophet's emphasis was clearly opposed to mere ritualistic sacrifices. He was negative about these. God requires His people to do justly, to love mercy and to walk humbly with Him. This is the tenor of all the prophetic voices in the Old Testament regarding social service and concern.

Jeremiah said, "His word was in mine heart as a burning fire shut up in my bones, and I was weary with forbearing, and I could not stay" (Jer. 20:9).

Social Ministry

The prophet did not hold back his message but proclaimed it frankly.

> Thus saith the Lord; Go down to the house of the king of Judah, and speak there this word, and say, Hear the word of the Lord, O king of Judah, that sittest upon the throne of David, thou, and thy servants, and thy people that enter in by these gates: Thus saith the Lord; Execute ye judgment and righteousness, and deliver the spoiled out of the hand of the oppressor: and do no wrong, do no violence to the stranger, the fatherless, nor the widow, neither shed innocent blood in this place. For if ye do this thing indeed, then shall there enter in by the gates of this house kings sitting upon the throne of David, riding in chariots and on horses, he, and his servants, and his people. But if ye will not hear these words, I swear by myself, saith the Lord, that this house shall become a desolation (Jer. 22:1-5).

Amos, the eighth-century prophet who came before Christ, cried loudly from the marketplace: "But let judgment run down as waters, and righteousness as a mighty stream" (Amos 5:24).

Isaiah called the people to righteousness with a remarkably sensitized social conscience: "Wash you, make you clean; put away the evil of your doings from before mine eyes; cease to do evil; learn to do well; seek judgment, relieve the oppressed, judge the fatherless, plead for the widow" (Isa. 1:16, 17).

A natural question would arise: "Does the New Testament contain social compassion like the Old Testament?" The answer is a resounding "Yes!" The heart of the Gospel is that "God so loved the world" (Jn. 3:16). The New Testament, like the Old, is acutely aware that there are satanic forces that are detrimental if not devastating to society. The New Testament teaching is that poverty (Lk. 6:20), war (Jas. 4:1), discrimination (Col. 3:11), superstition (Gal. 4:9), immorality (I Thess. 4:3), slavery (Rev. 18:11-13), and oppression (Mk. 10:42, 43) are all part of Satan's attempt to scuttle the human race and keep it from flowering under God.

Jesus' platform for ministry in society was profoundly brief and pungent. With amazing insight He enunciated that platform which still has the same pertinence:

> When he came to the village of Nazareth, his boyhood home, he went as usual to the synagogue on Saturday, and stood up to read the Scriptures. The book of Isaiah the prophet was handed to him, and he opened it to the place where it says: "The Spirit of the Lord is upon me; he has appointed me to preach Good News to the poor; he has sent me to heal the brokenhearted and to announce that captives shall be released and the blind shall see, that the downtrodden shall be freed from their oppressors, and that God is ready to give blessings to all who come to him." He closed the book and handed it back to the attendant and sat down, while

Social Ministry

everyone in the synagogue gazed at him intently. Then he added, *"These Scriptures came true today!"* (Lk. 4:16-21, TLB)

Significantly, when John the Baptist was imprisoned for his bold preaching and began to have second thoughts about Jesus' credentials and sent messengers saying, "Art thou he that should come, or do we look for another?" (Mt. 11:3), Jesus used the occasion to send back messengers saying,

> Go back to John and tell him all you have seen and heard here today: how those who were blind can see. The lame are walking without a limp. The lepers are completely healed. The deaf can hear again. The dead come back to life. And the poor are hearing the Good News (Lk. 7:22, TLB).

Here Jesus made His own case. It was not enough to be correct theologically in some abstract sense, but rather, His social action underscored His Messiahship. He went beyond that by virtually making social consciousness a basic plank in the faith of anyone who would follow Him. In Matthew 25:31-46 a lengthy passage cites His return to earth in glory at the end of the age. All the nations will be arrayed before the Savior and He will separate them one from another. Then He will say:

> Come, blessed of my Father, into the Kingdom prepared for you from the founding of the world.

> For I was hungry and you fed me; I was thirsty and you gave me water; I was a stranger and you invited me into your homes; naked and you clothed me; sick and in prison, and you visited me. Then these righteous ones will reply, "Sir, when did we ever see you hungry and feed you? Or thirsty and give you anything to drink? Or a stranger, and help you? Or naked, and clothe you? When did we ever see you sick or in prison, and visit you?" And I, the King, will tell them, "When you did it to these my brothers you were doing it to me!" (Mt. 25: 34-40, TLB)

He followed these important words by saying that if they were failing to be faithful in these things in their society, they also were failing to do them to the Savior. What more poignant, powerful, specific words could our Lord give than these to show that social service is a vital part of the Christian lifestyle?

When we add the apostles' teachings, particularly Paul's, to those of Jesus, we find that these committed men grappled with every kind of community issue. Political exploitation, military service, racial strife, consumption of food offered to idols, the position of women in the Church and in society, proper dress and modesty, relationships with non-Christians, taxation, prostitution, control of disease, relief of poverty, and obedience to the laws of the land were all mentioned by the apostles in their writings.

Social Ministry

Members of the Church of Jesus Christ, including the Baptist manifestation of this Church throughout the world, have given their lives to address themselves with love to these issues within society. They could not sit back and pluck decorously at the problems with delicate fingertips. Instead, they waded out into the middle of the mess and shared mankind's sufferings in the name of Christ. The result has been the founding of hospitals, orphanages, institutions for the poor, the elderly, and the mentally ill, as well as relief for the poverty-stricken. Historically, the Church's social conscience has created a beautiful although troubled chapter in its development. The alertness of early Baptists to the wrong of being taxed without representation, of paying for a religion they did not want which had been superimposed upon them by monarchs, and the willingness to die, if need be, to effect real life changes are some of the most encouraging aspects of Baptist history.

It is not easy to bless the lives of others unless we have been in their position of need. Thus it was that David Brainerd went to live with the Indians; William Booth lived in London's East End; and William Seagrave, a great Baptist surgeon, lived out his life, sick or well, in a village in Burma, serving that society's ills for Christ, and then sharing the Good News of salvation with his patients on his hospital rounds. He could hardly be pried away from Burma even for a rest, lest something would happen while he was away from his beloved Burmese.

THE BAPTIST HERITAGE

In earlier years James Keir Hardie established the Labor Party in England. Along with men like Wesley, he may well have preserved England from the fate of France and its revolution. Because of Hardie's Christian commitment, he could not see the laboring man being cheated out of his just rewards for his hard work. The Gospel was being proclaimed as he bargained for fairness in the courts of his homeland.

Wilberforce almost single-handedly brought about the abolition of slavery by England's Parliament after being profoundly influenced by the godly John Newton, who had been a slave ship captain prior to his conversion. Reciting the names of Christian workers, both within and outside the Baptist fold, emphasizes that wherever the Gospel is preached for the whole man, in his whole situation, social service plays a significant role in the life-style of these Christians.

Feeling hurt, bearing the burden, and sharing in other people's sufferings are part of the calling to which Baptists have responded. Amy Carmichael summed it up in her thought-provoking poem, "Hast Thou No Scar?"

> Hast thou no scar?
> No hidden scar on foot, or side, or hand?
> I hear thee sung as mighty in the land,
> I hear them hail the bright ascendant star,
> Hast thou no scar?

Social Ministry

Hast thou no wound?
Yet I was wounded by the archers, spent,
Leaned Me against a tree to die; and rent
By ravening beasts that compassed Me, I swooned:
Hast THOU no wound?

No wound? No scar?
Yet, as the Master shall the servant be,
And pierced are the feet that follow Me;
But thine are whole: can he have followed far
who has no wound nor scar?

A study of Baptist life-styles reveals that a few are convinced that today's world should write the agenda for the Church and that the Church should faithfully adhere to it. Yet, other Baptists would see the grace of Christ's Gospel as enabling them to be active *in* the world but not *of* the world. The believer who is in the world as God's man of hope and joy can be free to weep or rejoice with the world because it can neither give nor take away the hope and joy that Christ alone has given him. Therefore, social consciousness must entail the believer's being in the world, being sensitive to it, recognizing its problems and ministering to resolve and/or alleviate them. In his willingness to be used of God by relating to people evangelistically or at the point of their social needs, the believer must be concerned that he is not more religious than God nor more worldly than Jesus. That is, he must not attempt to over-organize, over-strategize, and otherwise encumber God's work in the effort to be "religious," nor must he seek to be part of the world beyond that which Christ manifested—in being willing to die for the world, yet, without becoming like it in its wicked godlessness.

The great tragedy of many believers has been their unwillingness to be informed and participating members of Christ's Body. They seem to prefer organizational structures, the clergy, and the accouterments that can be financially supported and encouraged without any personal involvement of their own talents and abilities. An old story says a lad came to his parents one evening and asked if they remembered "that valuable vase which we have handed down in our family from generation to generation?"

"Of course, I remember," said the mother. "Why do you ask?"

The boy replied with a frightened look, "Well, this generation has dropped it!" We dare not drop this valuable Gospel which God has placed in our hands. He expects us to be responsible in our relationships. This Gospel is a relational Gospel, relating men to one another and to Christ's Kingdom. We must relate to them, also, in the sharing process. We dare not fail.

Baptist history is filled with the lives of veritable saints of God who have faithfully shared the Gospel at great price—even death. Our life-style for the 20th and 21st centuries dares not manifest less.

Social Ministry

Questions for Thought and Discussion

1. Is the Gospel "political"? Does it carry implications for society and government and the political affairs of people and nations?
2. What do the Ten Commandments tell us about God's will for the social context of human life?
3. What does it mean to be "in the world but not of the world"?
4. What social needs and human problems are being neglected today by the Church or individual Christians?
5. What major contributions have the Baptists made to the heritage of the Church?
6. How are Baptists different from some of the major denominations in the Christian heritage?
7. What do Baptists share in common with all Christians?

Suggestions for Further Study

Torbet, *A History of the Baptists,* pp. 356-384, 470-486, 512-533.

APPENDIX

CHRONOLOGICAL REVIEW OF IMPORTANT DATES FOR BAPTISTS

The following significant Baptist happenings, along with many more which are unlisted, remind us of the trail for religious liberty which Baptists have helped blaze.

1600, July 24	Roger Williams baptized in England.
1638	John Clarke organized FBC, Newport, R. I.
1640, Feb. 29	Benjamin Keach born in England; revived congregational singing.
1644, Mar. 14	Roger Williams obtained charter for Providence.
1660, Nov. 12	John Bunyan jailed in England where he wrote *Pilgrim's Progress*.
1707, July 27	Association of Baptist Churches in U. S. A. organized at Philadelphia.

1740, Jan. 6	John Fawcett born in England; author of "Blest Be The Tie that Binds."
1761, Aug. 17	William Carey born in England; the parent of Baptist missionary work.
1774	Isaac Backus petitioned the Continental Congress for "Baptist Liberties in New England."
1775, May 20	George Lisle baptized; organized first church for Negroes in America and became first Baptist foreign missionary from America.
1788, Aug. 9	Adoniram Judson born in Mass.; became first white American missionary.
1789, Oct. 31	John Mason Peck born in Conn.; became first missionary to western U.S. and founder of ABHMS (BNM).

Appendix

1808, Oct. 21	Samuel Francis Smith born in Mass.; author of "My Country 'Tis of Thee," written while a student at Andover Newton.
1812, Sept. 6	Adoniram Judson baptized as a believer in India (Baptist).
1814, May 21	General Missionary Convention of Baptist Denomination in U.S.A. for Foreign Missions formed, later ABFMS, (Now BIM of ABC).
1824, Feb. 25	Baptist General Tract Society formed, (now BEM of ABC).
1833, July 31	Emancipation of slaves in Jamaica due to work of Baptist missionary, William Knibb.
1834, April 29	Joseph Henry Gilmore born in Mass.; author of "He Leadeth Me."

THE BAPTIST HERITAGE

1834, June 19	Charles Haddon Spurgeon born in England; became best-known preacher of the 19th century.
1845, May 8	Southern Baptist Convention formed at Augusta, Georgia.
1853, May 5	American Baptist Historical Society formed.
1871, April 3	Woman's American Baptist Foreign Missionary Society formed.
1886, Aug. 25	National Baptist Convention formed at St. Louis, Mo.
1891, May 23	First Chapel Car dedicated.
1895, Sept. 24	National Baptist Convention, U.S.A., organized in Atlanta.
1907, May 17	Northern Baptist Convention formed at Washington, D.C.

Appendix

1915, Sept. 9   National Baptist Convention of America, Unincorporated, organized in Chicago.

1961, Nov. 14   Progressive National Baptist Convention, Inc., formed at Cincinnati.